Act
Three

Create the Life You Want

After Your First Career

and Full-time Motherhood

JULIE SHIFMAN

GREENLEAF
BOOK GROUP PRESS

Published by Greenleaf Book Group Press
Austin, Texas
www.gbgpress.com

Distributed by Greenleaf Book Group LLC

For ordering information or special discounts for bulk purchases, please
contact Greenleaf Book Group LLC at PO Box 91869, Austin, TX 78709,
512.891.6100.

Design and composition by Greenleaf Book Group LLC
Cover design by Greenleaf Book Group LLC

Publisher's Cataloging-In-Publication Data
(Prepared by The Donohue Group, Inc.)
Shifman, Julie.
  Act three : create the life you want after your first career and full-time
motherhood / Julie Shifman. — 1st ed.
    p. : ill. ; cm.
  ISBN: 978-1-60832-364-7
    1. Middle-aged women—Employment re-entry—United States. 2. Middle-
aged women—Vocational guidance—United States. 3. Stay-at-home
mothers—United States. I. Title.
HF5382.6 .S55 2012
158.6   2012932339

Part of the Tree Neutral® program, which offsets the number of
trees consumed in the production and printing of this book by
taking proactive steps, such as planting trees in direct proportion to
the number of trees used: www.treeneutral.com

TreeNeutral®

Printed in the United States of America on acid-free paper

12 13 14 15 16 17   10 9 8 7 6 5 4 3 2

First Edition

Mid-Continent Public Library
15616 East US Highway 24
Independence, MO 64050

Contents

Acknowledgments

I HAVE TO BEGIN BY THANKING my wonderful husband of twenty-six years, Steve. Every day I feel lucky to be married to him and appreciate his encouragement of my ideas and his very helpful business acumen and advice. I also want to thank my family: my four boys/men (J., Jake, Alex, and Ari), my loving parents (Phil and Lois Cohen), and my wonderful in-laws (Morrey and Renae Shifman) for all their love and support over the years. I also want to thank all my many friends (like Lori, Suzy, Linda, Julie, Leslie, Louise, Beth, and Jane) whose quest for their own Act Three was the beginning of my impetus to found my company.

A big thank-you goes to all the inspirational women across the country who told me their Act Three stories. While I was able to profile only eleven of them in this book, I was inspired by them all and look forward to sharing the stories of other women through blogs, Facebook, and articles in the future. Thanks also to the many Act Three clients and the hundreds of survey women who revealed their very personal feelings and allowed me to share their thoughts in this book so that other women could learn from their experiences.

Finally, thanks go out to my excellent staff and coaches at Act Three, who every day help our clients find their more fulfilling Act Three.

Julie Shifman

Introduction

A pile of rocks ceases to be a pile when somebody contemplates it with the idea of a cathedral in mind.

—*Antoine de Saint-Exupéry*

IN 1957, 4.3 MILLION BABIES WERE born in the United States, the most babies born in any year before and a record that wasn't broken again until 2007. And those babies and other women born around that time (around 40 million) will be empty-nesting soon or already have. Research shows that this major life transition can be profoundly challenging for boomer women. Many will struggle to define their next stage of life. This struggle will be even more challenging for those women who took time off to stay home to raise their children. If you are one of these women, you are probably asking yourself, "Who am I now, and what can I do next?" Answering this question will ultimately lead to a more compelling and fulfilling next stage of life. And that is the purpose of this book: to guide you along the path to the fullest life possible in your Act Three—the stage that follows your first career (Act One) and full-time motherhood (Act Two).

But before we begin talking about your Act Three, I want to start by asking a question.

What does this picture look like to you? Does it look like some big rocks? . . . blocks of marble?

This is what it looked like to Michelangelo.

Michelangelo worked under the premise that the image of David was already fully formed in the block of marble. What this block of marble would become—in effect, its potential,— was always there. His

creativity merely recognized it, and his energy merely released it. You may be wondering what Michelangelo and this block of marble have to do with you. I'll explain shortly, but first I have to ask you a question.

Let's say that your life expectancy is eighty years. If you are forty-five, fifty, sixty, whatever age you are now, pretend that you are actually eighty years old and you are looking back at your life. Now imagine you continue doing all the things you are doing right now and doing them in the same way until you reach this pretend age of eighty. Take a minute to really think about this. Would the eighty-year-old you say that this was the life you wanted, that this life has been fulfilling, that you achieved to your potential, that you made the impact or left the legacy that you intended and desired? According to my research, if you are like many women, you would likely say no—and you wouldn't say it quietly; you'd shout it. These women feel they failed to release the potential within.

This feeling of wanting more out of life is artfully described by one woman:

> *I often worry about this. I have done some incredible things in my life. I have my family, many wonderful and caring friends, and have had some outstanding experiences. But I know I am going to look back on my life and be sad that I cared too much about what people thought and didn't take enough risks to do something that I really wanted to do.*

Even women who appear successful and totally confident may have these questioning feelings. Jane Fonda describes this so beautifully in her book *Prime Time*:

> *I realized then that it was not so much the idea of death itself that frightened me as it was being faced with regrets, the "what ifs" and the "if onlys" when there is no time left to do anything about them. I didn't want to arrive at the end of the Third Act and discover too late all that I had not done.*

And this takes us back to Michelangelo and his block of marble. You know, just like Michelangelo knew about the marble block, that there is great potential in you struggling to get out, but you haven't been able to define it or release it. For whatever reason, that hidden potential, that burning desire, is still buried beneath layers of rock. For some of you, the challenge is to imagine how your life could be different. You see other women doing all kinds of interesting things, but you just can't imagine what you might do.

Here is how one woman summed it up.

I'm approaching my thirtieth high school reunion next year. If I fall into the mind-set of comparing myself to other women I graduated from high school with, I in no way, shape, or form "measure up" to a majority of them. Demons are hard to shake off, and letting go of the past is equally difficult. Learning to look forward and not back is the biggest challenge I face as I figure out what it is I'm supposed to be doing next.

Maybe you imagine so many different things that you simply can't pick one. One day you imagine going back to school and becoming a social worker, and the next day you imagine getting your Pilates certification to teach at a health club. You end up doing neither, because for some reason stuff keeps getting in the way. Or maybe something is holding you back. You haven't been able to chip away at the marble and reveal its necessary and important parts—its essence.

Others of you can easily imagine exactly what you want to be doing, but for some reason you've just been talking and talking about it and never actually doing anything different. Imagining without doing is just plain daydreaming. I'm sure you know someone who always has a new idea or a new plan. Occasionally she acts on it, but then, the next time you talk to her she's already moved on to something else.

Whether you've yet to discover what you want out of your Act Three or have discovered it but aren't acting on it, either way you're treading water. You're not moving forward. For some people, I suppose, a life of treading water, of status quo, is fine. But my guess is that you wouldn't be reading this book if treading water was enough for you.

The key is to both imagine and then follow through and do it. This book will help you do both, as you move from having big dreams about your future to taking the first small steps toward making them reality.

MY STORY

I remember playing dress up when I was a little girl. My grandmother dressed me in her clothes, hats, and gloves and put makeup on me, and for some reason, she called me Mrs. Octopus (or at least that's what it sounded like to my four-year-old ears).

Julie, age four, playing dress-up

If I really think back, what I was doing was imagining; I loved everything about it. I imagined a time when I really would wear fancy clothes, and I created a made-up life that went along with the clothes. I had a

Julie, age fourteen, dancing ballet

made-up husband, made-up job, and made-up kids. In effect, as a child, I had a vision of the future I wanted.

In college, I had an even clearer vision for my future. I was going to be a professional ballet dancer. When I was young I spent most of my waking hours in ballet class. I lived and breathed ballet. I walked like a dancer (back held straight, head up, feet turned out) and wore my hair like a dancer (pulled up in a bun). I even watched TV like a dancer (sitting in the splits for hours, basically ripping out my hamstrings to be flexible). As a ballet major in college, I worked really hard toward the goal of becoming a professional dancer. But then at age twenty, in what I can only describe as one of the worst decisions of my life, I quit ballet cold turkey to follow a guy to Colorado.

Of course, my life didn't turn out remotely close to the vision I had imagined in college (picture Natalie Portman in *Black Swan*, without all the psychological nuttiness), but that's not the point. The point isn't whether the vision ended up being right. The point is that I had a vision.

But once I got older, as my kids were leaving the nest, I really struggled to imagine a different future. I felt lost. Here's what happened to me.

The guy I left my ballet dreams for turned out not to be too great of a guy. But the good news is that I went to law school in Colorado and briefly dated an amazing man until he moved away. And later, I moved to New York City to practice law and re-met that amazing man. He became my husband. As they say in Yiddish, it was *beshert*—meant to be.

Right after we got married, I got pregnant. My husband and I were Midwesterners, and we struggled to picture raising this baby in our tiny apartment in New York City. So I quit my law job when I was nine months pregnant, and we moved to Cincinnati. I went back to work when my son was six months old and was lucky enough to find a part-time legal position (part time was pretty much unheard of in the mid-eighties). And then I got pregnant again, and then I got pregnant again, and then I got pregnant again. We ended up with four sons in five and a half years. I actually became a partner in my law firm while working part time in between sons number three and four. (I remember trying to keep my pregnancy with son number four a secret until the day after the partnership vote, sucking in my stomach as much as a pregnant stomach could be sucked in on a fourth pregnancy.) I went to work full time when my youngest was six months old. Even though this period of time was hectic—four small boys in various stages of diapers, preschool, and elementary school—it actually was manageable, with lots of help.

But then my four sons became teenagers (one with significant learning issues), and it wasn't so easy any longer to juggle all the demands. And the reality was that I didn't love my job anymore. But could I really just walk away? I had invested a huge amount of time and money to get to where I was. I earned a very good living. And I have to admit, I liked the recognition that came with saying I was a partner at a large law firm. (This was a time when a woman partner at a large law firm was still pretty rare.) If I left my partnership, it would be next to impossible to ever go back. So if I left, it was for good.

Julie and family, 2010

But I knew that I didn't want to spend the rest of my life practicing law, and with that realization, I walked away. I loved being at home—excluding the time my oldest son was suspended from high school, and when my youngest son broke his kneecap in a baseball game in Florida and I was the only mother who hadn't traveled down from Ohio with the team. And I really enjoyed the time it afforded me to get more involved in the community. I even had time to work out and to return to my first love, ballet.

Then my oldest son went off to college, and I started asking the nagging question: What was I going to do next with my life? I knew that I didn't want to and couldn't go back to law. So with one possibility ruled out, I still had thousands of other possibilities to consider and no real idea how to figure it out. Who could help a well-educated former professional who had been home raising children and now needed help figuring out what she wanted to do—and could do—next?

So with no real plan, no real understanding of my talents, and no real guidance, I jumped around, trying lots of different things to see if one would stick. First, I started a consulting company to work with family-owned businesses. I discovered that I was good at sales (getting clients) but that I didn't enjoy dealing with what often seemed to me irrational behavior. I learned that being in business with your family can turn even the most rational person temporarily insane.

I closed that business and began a consulting company to work with nonprofit organizations. This, I conjectured at the time, would mean working with people and causes I really liked. These were great people and great projects, but I hadn't considered how few nonprofits could actually afford to hire me. At the same time, I got certified to teach the New York City Ballet Exercise Workout and taught that at various fitness clubs around town. This was fun, and I was using my dance background, but it clearly wasn't a long-term or profitable solution.

At one point I even approached my husband about working in his chemical business. I didn't do this because I really wanted to work in a chemical business or to even work with him (see above about becoming insane when working with family); I did it because I didn't know what I wanted. Having him give me a job seemed like the easy way out. Thankfully, he graciously declined.

Through all this, I came to discover that I wasn't the only woman struggling with these issues. It seemed as if all my friends were wrestling with the same problems. Take Janet, for example. She graduated from college with a degree in business and started selling office equipment. She was one of the top salespeople for her company for several years in a row. During this time, her husband's career was also taking off. When she had a son, they were able to make it work, even if it was a struggle. But then baby number two, a daughter, came along, and at the same time, her husband was promoted, resulting in him traveling significantly more. Most of the child care and all the household duties fell to Janet. As she tells it,

Something had to give. Once when I dropped off my daughter at day care, I realized that she didn't have shoes on (and this was in the middle of winter!). I knew then that I was trying to do too much.

And the reality was that we could afford to live on my husband's salary, so why was I putting our family through so much stress just so I could have a job that I really didn't love? I took what I thought was going to be a short-term hiatus from work. I figured I would go back when my daughter was in kindergarten. Here I am fifteen years later, and I am not happy where I am. I feel like there is a lot more that I could, or even should be doing, but I just don't know what to do. I don't even know if I want to go back to work. Giving up my flexibility when we don't really need the money would be really hard. And if I did go back to work, what would I be qualified to do? I obviously can't go back to what I did before. They don't even make those copiers anymore. I feel like this is so hard to figure out that I just keep complaining but doing nothing.

My friend Janet was just one example. It seemed as if most of my time with friends—walks, lunches, book club meetings—all devolved into the discussion of "What are we going to do next?" But other than talk to each other about this, none of us really knew how to get help. Who could help women like Janet, who had been home with children for ten, fifteen, even twenty years and were ready to figure out what was next?

I decided I could be the one to help. Through much research and by conducting several focus groups, I discovered that my friends and I are part of a very large demographic. This is the first time in history that large numbers of highly educated women (the baby boomers), who had interesting careers before they chose to stay home to raise their children, are empty-nesting. According to my research, some of these women do want to go back to work or start businesses (about 35 percent). But about 65 percent don't; they just want to make sure that their next stage of life, their Act Three, will be interesting and productive.

Through the research I did, I also uncovered many of the challenges these women face, and I've continued to uncover them in a recent survey I conducted with hundreds of women across the country. Some of these challenges are obvious. Well over half of the women I heard from were struggling to figure out what they wanted to do. And for those women who wanted to return to work, it was also challenging for them to figure out what they were qualified to do with such a long gap in their work history.

After this research and listening to so many women share their thoughts and concerns, I started to formulate a concept for what I personally wanted to do next. I would create a company that would help women like me figure out what they wanted to do next. I would get my coaching certification so I could coach the women. And then I would write a book so that all the women my company couldn't personally touch could also get help. My Act Three would be helping women achieve their own Act Threes.

I branded the company Act Three because I think it accurately reflects the place these women want to be. Act One was their first career. Act Two was raising their children, an important and fulfilling part of their lives that should never be discounted. But now many want an interesting and challenging Act Three, statistically the longest of their three acts. (Women who are forty-five today should live healthy lives well into their eighties.)

So here we are today. We've helped hundreds of women through our seminars, workshops, and individual coaching to discover their Act Three—whether that means starting a business, going back to work, or focusing on a cause they care about. Now, with this book, we can help you, too.

This book follows the systematic process we use to help our clients, and each chapter is one step in that process. I start by first helping you to imagine the possibilities for your Act Three, to identify your passions, gifts, and motivations. Once we've narrowed those down and looked at some options that might work for you, I share the techniques and suggestions that have changed the lives of so many of my clients. I show you how to prepare for change, how to take small steps, how to identify the things that might be holding you back, and how to persevere through the inevitable setbacks you'll face.

In each chapter, I also profile a remarkable woman who exemplifies the principle outlined in the chapter. Most of these women are just

DREAMING BIG

↓

DISCOVERING YOUR GIFTED PASSIONS

↓

UNDERSTANDING YOUR MOTIVATIONS

↓

THE POWER EQUATION:
COMBINING PASSIONS AND MOTIVATIONS

↓

VISUALIZING SUCCESS

↓

GETTING IN CHANGE SHAPE

↓

LAUNCHING AND LEARNING

↓

TAKING SMALL STEPS

↓

CREATING A PORTFOLIO CAREER

↓

IDENTIFYING WHAT'S HOLDING YOU BACK

↓

PERSEVERING THROUGH SETBACKS

↓

ARRIVAL

Julie speaking at an Imagine . . . Then Do It women's conference

like you; they're not celebrities. I wanted to interview women you could relate to. I know you will enjoy meeting and getting to know all of them. An award-winning documentarian, a nationally syndicated radio host, a fitness guru, and volunteers changing the lives of thousands—these women are all living Act Three to its fullest. They inspired me, and I know they'll inspire you, too. At the end of each chapter, I also hand over exercises and tools that will help you apply what you've learned to your own life, right away.

Let's get started with the first step: having big dreams for your future and opening up the possibilities for your Act Three.

ONE

Dreaming Big

Imagination is the beginning of creation.
You imagine what you desire; you will what you imagine;
and at last you create what you will.

—George Bernard Shaw

REMEMBER THE FIRST WORDS OF THE song "Do-Re-Mi"—"Let's start at the very beginning, a very good place to start"? Let's take that advice from Rodgers and Hammerstein and start at the very beginning of your journey toward an incredible Act Three: learning to dream big and opening your mind to any and all possibilities.

Amy Sewell wasn't afraid to dream big when she accepted a rather mundane story assignment from a community paper—she was to do a feature on a local elementary school dance program. Amy, a former marketing executive and stay-at-home mom living in New York City, took the writing gig after wrestling with the realization that her twin girls didn't need her as much as they once had. The spirited kids she met on the assignment planted a big dream in her imagination. Two years later, her dream became one of the top grossing documentaries of its time, *Mad Hot Ballroom*.

AMY'S STORY

Though she led a happy life, Amy Sewell was having breakdowns behind the closed doors of her New York City apartment. Her twin teenage girls no longer needed her like they once did, and she was wrestling with what to do next: More kids? A new career? When she

Young Amy and her husband, Charlie, traveling around the world

and her husband at last decided that, given Amy's age and the amount of space they had living in the city, two was the perfect number of children, Amy knew she needed a new outlet. She needed more in her life.

Amy had always been good at writing, so one day she got up the nerve to approach the editor of her neighborhood's monthly community newspaper and ask for an assignment. She was given the unglamorous task of covering the fifth-grade class at the neighborhood elementary school who were learning to ballroom dance and competing in the big city-wide competition. She was proud to be paid ten

cents per word. It was hardly breaking news, but from the moment she walked into that fifth-grade classroom, Amy started dreaming big.

As she followed the fifth graders for a semester, gathering material for her 1,500-word article, Amy kept having a nagging thought. "I was always thinking, this story would be better told visually," says Amy. "And it never went away. You know when you have ten ideas, and

one won't leave you alone? It becomes a child in your brain who's constantly tapping your shoulder, saying, 'Yoo-hoo, when are you going
to take care of me?'" An idea had taken hold of Amy, and her imagination ran with it. "It was the germ of a big idea, and she wouldn't let
go." (Amy's ideas are always female, she explains.)

The turning point came one night when Amy was home with her
husband. She turned to him and said, "I'm going to make a documentary about these kids." As she verbalized it, she realized she had offi-
cially set things in motion. Naturally, both of them had doubts about
how she'd make a documentary, particularly considering she had never
done anything like it before, but Amy refused to let obstacles block her
imagination. She immediately started researching and planning.

One of the biggest hurdles she encountered was one that stunts the
dreaming process for many people: money. Amy knew she would need
a lot of it. As she filmed and edited footage of the vivacious fifth graders learning to tango and cha-cha on their way to the big competition,

Amy and Marilyn Agrelo, the director of Mad Hot Ballroom

the bills piled up. She had to call investors and ask for more and more funds. It was stressful and scary at times, but through it all, Amy kept her dream front and center—to make an entertaining film that also highlighted the importance of the arts in education, a cause she felt passionate about. She balanced the larger purpose of spreading the importance of arts education through her documentary with the risk of losing the money if the project failed. But through all the pressure, she had faith that she could pull off a top-tier documentary. Money wouldn't stop her. As Amy says, "People shouldn't be irresponsible with their mortgages or livelihoods, but if you find something that has a larger purpose, money shouldn't be the reason to stop you."

Amy also had personal obstacles that threatened to shut down her dream. Though her twins were older, they and her husband still relied on Amy around the house. And after *Mad Hot Ballroom* was released and started gaining in popularity and getting praise from around the world, her relationship with her husband went through a bit of shakiness. Amy was flying first-class out to Los Angeles on a Paramount jet, and her spouse couldn't help wondering what was going on in her new world and whether she'd stay around. For Amy, one of the great things about following her dream at that stage in her life was that the trappings of success weren't that important to her, and she was able to keep a level head as she balanced the praise and premieres with her priority of maintaining a healthy relationship with her husband of nineteen years.

Mad Hot Ballroom went on to receive many awards and was the ninth-largest-grossing documentary of all time. The experience changed Amy so much that she wrote a book about it, in part hoping to inspire other stay-at-home moms to imagine all the things they could achieve. One of Amy's greatest lessons to all of us is that she thinks of the dreaming process as a jump from a ledge: "You're standing on a cliff, and the only thing that keeps you from jumping to greatness are all these things plugged into your back: people, negativity, labels, things you think you can't do. When you sever those and jump, there is only space in front of you." It's in that space that all kinds of new experiences can happen.

Amy in front of a movie theater showing her second film

For Amy, the process of opening up incredible possibilities for the future is ongoing. Even though she's made a hit film in her third act, she's still thinking about what's next: "I don't know where I'm headed, but I know my eyes are open. And for me, I have to stick the knife in and twist and feel some pain and then head off in a new direction." The dreaming never stops.

Amy got some of her inspiration to keep dreaming and growing from Gloria Steinem, whom she interviewed for her second documentary, *What's Your Point, Honey?* (on the women's liberation movement). Amy asked Steinem what her greatest achievement was. Steinem replied that she hadn't made her greatest achievement yet. "I interviewed her when she was seventy-five," says Amy, "and her plan was to live to one hundred, so she felt she had all these years left to keep doing incredible things. That was a wake-up call for me, because I thought, if I live to one hundred, I've got fifty-two years left. I can go to law school, I can become a teacher, I can learn to surf, I can do almost anything." Now that's what I call dreaming big.

LEARNING TO DREAM BIG

I hope that you are as inspired by Amy as I am. Now it's time for you to learn to dream big just like she did.

It's likely that you're struggling with mentally opening up the possibilities for your future. I surveyed moms from across the country, and when asked if they wanted to do something different, a significant majority responded that they wanted to do something new, wanted to change their lives, but had no idea what to do differently. They were, in effect, stuck from a lack of imagination—not moving forward or even sideways. And many of those women actually said they were resigned to believing that nothing could really help them. Here are two poignant responses to the survey.

> The double whammy of empty nest and menopause really affects my state of mind. As a not-quite-sixty-year-old, the contempla-tion of "Who am I?" is daunting and emotional and frustrating. What do I want my life to be, apart from the context provided by the people I love?

◦∽

> Now that my kids don't need me as much, I don't know what I should or could be doing. And I'm really struggling to figure it out, but I know I don't want others to just say, "She is a darn good tennis player!"

So how do you go about imagining what your Act Three will look like? We'll spend the next several chapters helping you do that. But the very first step is to relax, take a deep breath, and recognize that figuring out your next step may take a while. Start by realizing that you won't conceive a new life plan overnight. Let's face it—it took you maybe forty, fifty, sixty years to get to where you are today, and you shouldn't expect to find a new direction in a few months.

Amy Sewell told me she doesn't believe that change can happen overnight. As she explains, "We often have expectations that we will have a new direction in a month or six months, but we have to let go of that. It could be three years; it could be ten years." Once you're comfortable with the fact that your Act Three might take a while— and that it's not something that can be rushed—then you might as well relax and enjoy the thrill of exploration. As you allow yourself to imagine the future and come up with those big dreams, think of it as a gift to yourself. At this point in your life, you have time to explore, to figure out who you really are and what you really want out of the rest of your life.

If step one in the dreaming-big process is allowing yourself the luxury of time, step two is to completely open your mind to all possibilities—and I do mean *all* possibilities. You never know when one of those far-out ideas could end up being your next step forward. Easier said than done, I know, as so many of us have that little voice in our head that immediately closes down new ideas: *Well, that can't happen because . . .* or *That would cost way too much . . .* But when you're in the dreaming-big stage, there's absolutely no negative thinking allowed! You'll have plenty of opportunities later in the book to test your ideas against reality. But, and I can't emphasize this enough, if you let negativity—or even what you consider to be realistic objections—come in at this stage, then some of your best ideas will be shot down before you even give them the chance to develop.

And although you may be bursting at the seams with ideas for projects and initiatives after your first imagination session, I recommend that you keep these fledgling ideas to yourself for now. Don't share them with anyone. For those of us who like to share all our thoughts with our best friends or husband, it will be challenging to hold back. It is far too easy for others, even when they're trying to be supportive, to shoot down creative ideas with what they may feel is helpful advice. Plus, there are always people who, purposefully or inadvertently, subtly try to prevent those around them from succeeding. This behavior, while unfortunate, is a fact of life and a good reason for not sharing fledgling ideas.

For example, one client, Joanne, loved wine and had been dreaming about becoming a sommelier. But every time she mentioned it to her husband, he would challenge her, pointing out how unrealistic it was. So Joanne decided to forget about pursuing that dream. While we were working through Joanne's imagining stage together, she hesitantly brought up her idea about becoming a sommelier. We immediately began exploring all of the reasons she wanted to do this, why it seemed so interesting to her. Because we were dreaming big, we weren't worried about whether it made sense or was realistic. It didn't matter whether she had the right skill set, the right background, or the ability to have a sommelier's lifestyle. I told Joanne that there would be plenty of time later to determine whether being a sommelier was a real possibility for her.

It's so important to let your mind run free in this first stage. Even if it turns out that becoming a sommelier won't work for Joanne, the exercise of exploration could easily lead her to other ideas that may, in fact, work. And if Joanne comes up with a dream that really captures her imagination and sparks something inside her, it's possible that she'll find a way around the problems she thinks limit her. Joanne needs to give the sommelier idea the time to percolate, and you need to do the same thing, even with your most outrageous ideas. If they're shot down from the start, you couldn't possibly know if they could work for you or what other ideas might evolve from them. So keep your mind open, and don't talk about your ideas!

Amy Sewell told me that she is looking for new directions again (after three documentaries), and her first step is to avoid pigeonholing herself based on who people think she is. "People call me and they say, 'You're a filmmaker,' or 'You're a writer,' and I have to get rid of all that and kind of start over. And to do that I've got to make myself invisible almost and let myself go in new directions with no presumption of where I'm going. It's almost like throwing all your ideas up into the air and watching them fall in slow motion. You just don't know where they're going to land."

That's a great way to think about your first step toward Act Three. You've got to get rid of any preconceived notions of who you are or who people think you are, and then take any and all ideas you have for your future, throw them high up into the air, and see where they land.

EXERCISES FOR DREAMING BIG

Now on to the specifics of exactly *how* to open your mind to possibilities. For some of us, imagining comes naturally—it's basically daydreaming with a sense of purpose. But for others, people who tend to see in black and white, the "seeing is believing" type of person, this can be really challenging.

Regardless of which camp you find yourself in, try out these exercises to help you open your mind to possibilities. You don't have to do all of them—maybe start by picking a few to try. If you like working out or meeting people, try those exercises. If you like reading and writing, do those. Several of them involve writing, so you may want to invest in a nice journal and a good pen to consolidate your exercises. Don't expect to know exactly what you want to do after finishing these exercises. They are simply tools to open your mind to all possibilities. When you open your mind, eventually the right ideas will come to you.

1. VISUALIZE YOUR PERFECT DAY

Get out a piece of paper and a pen (I find this actually works better than typing on the computer). Picture an ideal day six years in the future. Think about that day as if you are actually living it, being as specific as possible. It may help to close your eyes so you can really visualize it. Picture how each hour of this ideal day would be spent.

For example, one client of mine wrote this for her visualization exercise: "I get up with the sun and take my dog for a run. We have moved out of our big house into a condo by the river, so we run along the boardwalk. I come back and read the paper while drinking my coffee as my husband goes off to work. I shower and get dressed and head to an office where I am working with interesting people on issues that I feel can make a difference. I have confidence in my skills which make me proud of myself. I am interacting with other adults, and we enjoy a great humorous rapport. I have lunch with a friend and check in on the phone with my daughter and grandchildren. After several more challenging hours at the office, I meet my husband for a wine tasting followed by seeing the symphony perform."

Now you try. Spend thirty minutes thinking and writing about that ideal day.

2. TRY THINGS ON FOR SIZE

Think about the last time you needed a really special dress. Perhaps this caused you to pay more attention to what some other women were wearing and even to notice pretty dresses in magazines and on TV, dresses you would've ignored had you not been in the market for one. Maybe you even hired an expert fashion consultant to give you advice. You probably went to different stores to try on many different dresses, certainly not believing that there was only one dress in the whole world. You knew there were lots of possibilities.

Think about the imagining stage as if you are looking for that special dress. Look for ideas everywhere around you: in the newspaper, on TV, on the Internet. Pay attention to everything you see and experience while traveling. Listen to what your friends are talking about. The idea for my company, Act Three, came from listening to my friends, many of whom were wondering (actually, I was too) what they were going to do next. I figured that if we were questioning, maybe a lot of other women were too. And voilà, there was a market niche for a new business.

You'll find that once you're actively looking for new ideas, new ideas will come to you. Be sure to carry a pad in your purse or to take notes on your phone as ideas come to you. You may be standing in line at the grocery store when an idea hits. Though you think you'll remember it, it's quite possible that by the time you get home ten other things have happened to you and you have forgotten your good idea.

At the end of a month (and I do suggest waiting this long), pull out your list of ideas and try them on for size. Close your eyes and picture doing each one individually. As you visualize, think about how each one makes you feel—happy, contented, energized? Does one just "feel right" to you? Write down all of your thoughts about each idea, but again, only write down the good thoughts.

3. INTERVIEW PEOPLE ABOUT WHAT THEY DO AND WHY THEY LIKE / DON'T LIKE IT

Have you ever seen a T-shirt with the saying "But enough of me talking about me, now you talk about me"? I've always found that shirt so funny since we all know people whose favorite topic of conversation is themselves. But you can actually put that to good use. Even people who aren't self-absorbed feel flattered if you ask them about themselves. It's a rare person who won't be flattered by your request, and, in fact, you will probably end up knowing far more than you ever wanted to about the person's life. Pick people who seem to you to be leading fulfilled lives. Then play the part of a good reporter. Find out how they spend their time, what they like and don't like about what they are doing, and—most important—how they got to where they are. Immediately after each conversation, write down your thoughts and reactions and anything they said that was particularly interesting. When you have interviewed several people, look through your notes and see if there are any common themes or patterns.

4. ASK YOURSELF, "WHAT WOULD I DO IF I KNEW FOR SURE I COULDN'T FAIL?"

This simple question has unleashed a lot of powerful ideas. We'll spend a lot of time later in the book talking about the fear of failure and how to overcome it, but at the imagination stage, you can put the prospect of failure aside and think, "If I were absolutely sure I couldn't fail, that I was going to be successful, what would I choose to do?"

Would you choose to be a sommelier, like Joanne, or an author or TV reporter or a politician? Be sure to write down your answer to this question.

5. READ ABOUT OTHER PEOPLE AND CURRENT EVENTS

To help you get a completely new perspective, pick up newspapers and magazines you wouldn't normally read. If you typically read your local paper each morning, try reading the *Wall Street Journal* for two weeks. If you read *O: The Oprah Magazine*, try *Inc.* or *Health* magazine, anything different. Even if—particularly if, in fact—your first reaction is "I probably won't like it." After each issue, ask yourself these questions and write down your thoughts: Did anything surprise me?

Did anything make me laugh or smile? Did anything make me mad? Did anything make me cry? If you answered yes to any of these questions, why did you feel those emotions? Did you read about an idea or topic that you want to learn more about? If so, by all means continue the exploration. Spend an hour or two at your computer researching that topic. At the end of the month, go back over all of the comments you wrote down, and look to see if there are any common themes. For example, did you find that you were always moved by articles or stories about children with disabilities? If so, that's something to pay attention to.

6. ATTEND EVENTS, LECTURES, AND PARTIES YOU WOULDN'T NORMALLY ATTEND

Dreaming big is about stepping out of your normal mode of existence to imagine what's possible. To help you do that, actively seek out events you normally wouldn't consider going to. This is similar to changing your reading habits in the previous exercise. It's all too easy to get stuck in ruts and tired routines, so keep an eye out for lectures, parties, benefits, and other events, particularly if they are based around topics you're interested in or causes that are important to you. Stepping out and doing something new puts you into fruitful territory for uncovering new ideas. And the best part about putting yourself at new types of events is the people you meet.

When you meet new people, be sure to ask them about themselves, particularly what they like or don't like about what they do. (And by "what they do," I don't necessarily mean do for a living—I mean how they live their lives.) And then, in the exercise above, after you attend each of these events, ask yourself what you learned and how you felt about it. If there was something particularly interesting, spend some time researching it. Record all your thoughts as soon as you are able to after the event. If you wait too long, your initial thoughts could be forgotten or you may find yourself discounting your initial reaction. At the end of the month, go back over your notes again looking for any common themes. Did you really enjoy meeting a certain kind of person or attending a certain kind of event? For example, were you fascinated when you attended a lecture series by women writers? Explore exactly why something was fascinating to you.

7. WRITE IN A JOURNAL

Every day, try to write in a journal for fifteen minutes. Some people find that first thing in the morning works best—before life gets in the way. Others think that right before bed is a great time for creative thinking. Whatever you decide, pick a time that works best for you and stick to that time. Doing so will help you form a new habit that becomes part of your day.

Finding a method of writing that you find enjoyable will also help you make writing a daily habit. Try writing on your laptop or tablet, and then try writing with a pen and paper. Discover what feels best for you.

There are no specific topics that you should write about, no right or wrong answers. Simply write down whatever comes into your mind at that moment. Be sure to record and pay particular attention to the things you enjoyed throughout the day. This process of recording your thoughts creates all kinds of new ideas. At the end of the month, when you have about thirty days' worth of material, look through all that you have written. Note whether any common themes jump out, particularly themes that make you happy.

Dayna Steele, a small-business owner you will meet in chapter 9, used this method to find her new direction in life. She realized she was no longer enjoying running her business. Not knowing where to turn for her next chapter, she recorded her thoughts before she went to bed every night for six weeks. At the end of the six weeks, she was surprised to see that the things that gave her the most pleasure were doing laundry, going to the grocery store, hanging out with her husband and kids, and doing consulting projects on the side. This information freed her to finally sell her business (after six months of hard financial planning) and devote her life to creating a portfolio career (which we will discuss in chapter 9).

8. TAKE A WALK, RIDE A BIKE, OR GO FOR A SWIM

Set aside time every day to get out and move. Do it by yourself, with no distractions. No talking on the cell phone or listening to music. Walking, biking, and swimming are some of the most common ways to get out and move, but maybe you have your own way. Perhaps you like to rollerblade or do yoga. For lots of people, the mere act of moving can release new creativity and ideas. I know I do my best thinking when I swim. There are no phones ringing or people talking or music playing to distract me. It's just me and my thoughts.

As you're walking, biking, swimming, or doing your own type of solo activity, let yourself daydream. Focus on letting your mind wander, as paradoxical as that sounds. Then, as soon as you get home, write down the thoughts that occurred to you while you were in motion. At the end of the month, look through all that you have written. Note any common themes that jump out, particularly ones that make you happy.

⌐∽

Now that you have opened your mind to the extraordinary possibilities that lie before you and worked hard at silencing your inner critic, you have given yourself the gift of picturing the ultimate Act Three. It probably won't come about just as you now see it, but the imagination process is the critical launching point. The next step is identifying your Gifted Passions.

TWO

Discovering Your Gifted Passions

We must be willing to let go of the life we planned so as to have the life waiting for us.

—Joseph Campbell

NOW THAT YOU HAVE SOME BIG ideas, it's time to get a little more focused. In this chapter we will do this by figuring out what I call your "Gifted Passions."

Anne Heyman was able to harness her passions and today is helping hundreds of African orphans survive. A stay-at-home mom in New York City, Anne was attending a lecture on the millions of orphans in Rwanda. She turned to her husband and said, "I have to do something about this," and just five years later she has created an entire youth village in Rwanda for more than five hundred orphans, complete with dorms, schools, and health care.

ANNE'S STORY

Anne Heyman spent her formative years in Cape Town, South Africa. A star table-tennis player, she grew up in a traditional Jewish household. When she was fifteen, her family left Africa for Boston. Little did Anne know that the third act of her life would take her back to Africa, where her gifts and passions would change the lives of countless people.

After going to college in Philadelphia—her focus was Third World politics, a thread she'd pick up again later—Anne went to law school and then became an assistant district attorney in Manhattan, where she lived with her husband. While living the hectic life of a DA, she had her first two kids, successfully juggling a burgeoning workload with the joys of motherhood. But when the prospect of a third child came along, Anne knew she wanted more time with her kids. Without a second thought, she left criminal law behind to focus on the ins and outs of raising three young children.

Though Anne had loved her job, she didn't miss work. Still, the shift to stay-at-home mom presented difficulties. Anne had a feeling that so many women know: she was now defined by whose mom or whose wife she was. "I remember going to business dinners with my husband," says Anne, "and when people asked what I did and I answered, 'I stay home with my kids,' they'd turn their back and walk off, because I couldn't possibly have anything interesting to say."

Fortunately, Anne had no difficulty building a new, post-DA identity for herself, centered on one-on-one time with her kids, morning horse rides, and philanthropic work. When her serial-entrepreneur husband had a few businesses up and running, the couple poured more resources into philanthropy and started a family foundation.

The kids of Agahozo-Shalom

The foundation put on a lecture series called "Moral Voices," and it was at one of these lectures, at Tufts University in 2005, that Anne had a series of life-altering realizations.

As the speaker outlined the atrocities surrounding the 1994 Rwandan genocide, Anne's thoughts stuck on one number: 1.2 million, the number of orphans in Rwanda. The word *genocide*, too, haunted her. She had been brought up in a Jewish home, spent a year in Israel, and had been actively involved with Jewish youth movements, so it wasn't a word that fell lightly on her ears.

That's when the pieces started to fall together. Anne knew there was a way to handle overwhelming orphan populations—it had happened in Israel in the middle of the twentieth century, after the Holocaust. *There's a solution for the orphan problem that exists in the world*, said a calm but insistent voice in her head. She knew she had to determine how they'd solved the problem in Israel and bring the same solution to

Rwanda. Her kids were older by that time—two in high school, one in middle school—and when she told her husband what she wanted to do but that she had no idea how she'd get it done, he said simply, "You're the one to do this."

In the following weeks, Anne researched youth villages and threw her idea at anyone who would listen. "Great idea!" was the inevitable response, but no one knew how to take it further. Then Anne stumbled upon Yemin Orde, a youth village tucked into the Carmel Mountains of northern Israel. She called the village's director, Chaim Peri, and he invited her to come to Israel to talk about the idea.

Caught up in the passion of her vision, Anne boarded a plane to Israel with a friend, Tina, who'd been so moved by Anne's idea that she quit her job to help. In Yemin Orde, Anne found the model she was looking for. It was the match that would light the fire under Anne's idea. After she and Tina took a short exploratory trip to Rwanda, she was more convinced than ever that setting up a youth village was the best way she could help the million-plus orphans of the devastated country. Though she couldn't help wondering whether the model would work, or even be embraced by Rwandans, she pressed on.

Combining her passion—for human rights issues, for Africa, and for the notion of *tikkun olam*, the Jewish obligation to repair the world—with her legal training and her planning and organization skills, Anne set about bringing her vision to life. She started by calling anyone and everyone she thought might know someone in Rwanda. Soon she'd put together a Rwandan advisory board, taken them to see Yemin Orde, and put together a team of Rwandan builders and architects to construct the village.

Anne started her project in September 2006. They broke ground in August 2007 and moved in their first group—125 kids—in December 2008. Today, the Agahozo-Shalom youth village includes a state-of-the-art school attended by 500 kids, a dining hall that seats 800 people, and a large community center. The village is also a farming community powered by the most effective modern farming techniques,

The village of Agahozo-Shalom

including greenhouses run by computers and drip-irrigation systems. The kids at Agahozo-Shalom pass along what they've received from Anne, doing community service that literally saves lives. They plant crops, build homes, work in the medical clinic, and mentor younger village residents. "They are very aware of the fact that they are lucky and privileged to have found themselves at the village, and that comes with an obligation to give back to their community," says Anne.

Agahozo-Shalom, the fruit of Anne's combined passions and gifts, is like a feedback loop of positivity for everyone who encounters it. Beyond feeding and sheltering abandoned and orphaned children, it empowers those children to give back to others. It enriches the lives of the many volunteers who give their time to the village. And it's serving as a shining example of how the youth village model can be applied elsewhere, something that gives Anne great hope.

Anne spends many days and sleepless nights worrying about the village and the responsibility she feels for the children. "I always tell people and myself that I go to bed at night knowing that I did the most

Anne speaking at the village

that I could do. Even if it doesn't work at the end of the day, I did what I could, and that has to be enough. When you think about getting involved in something and it being overwhelming—yes, the world's needs are overwhelming—but does that mean you don't do anything?

"I think it's much more logical and better for you as a person to say, 'Let me do what I can do.'"

When Anne meets women who say they don't have the kind of passion it takes to carry out such an audacious project, she patiently explains that it doesn't work that way. "Five years ago, I wouldn't have said that I was passionate about rescuing kids in need. I've learned that to find something that you're passionate about, don't wait for the passion. If there's something that interests you, find a little niche where you can do a little something."

Anne found her niche, one that lay at the intersection of her passions and skills. "I take great comfort in the fact that my life has meant something. Not that it wouldn't have if I had just had a husband, or just a career, or just kids. But I feel I've had the ability to make a difference, and I stood up and didn't walk away."

FINDING YOUR GIFTED PASSIONS

As you're thinking about all the possibilities for your third act, you may find yourself overwhelmed. Dreaming big, as you learned to do in the last chapter, expands your mind and opens you to the incredible scope of your own potential, but without a way to narrow down your dreams, you can get stuck. To keep yourself from jumping around from one idea to the next, you need to find what I call your "Gifted Passions"—the fruitful spot that lies at the intersection of your interests and your abilities.

Anne Heyman found that place by drawing together a set of gifts and passions that at first glance don't seem to add up to anything specific. She had a love for Africa, plus a passion for human rights and charity work, which she'd inherited as part of her Jewish upbringing. She also had a lot of legal know-how built up in her early career and a knack for incremental project management. By pursuing her interests, Anne stumbled upon a project that she was particularly suited for: her vision of the Rwandan youth village was an elegant synthesis of what she loved and what she was good at.

Your challenge, of course, is to do the same: find that synthesis of what you love and are good at.

Uncovering Your Passions

Finding your passions is the first step. Some women, particularly those who have been out of the workforce for more than ten years, struggle to come up with things they love to do. But I'm certain that no matter who you are, there's *something* you're passionate about, even if it's lying in wait, only partially discovered. Start with looking at what makes you happy throughout the day. Maybe it's writing, like Amy Sewell from chapter 1, or maybe it's gardening, like Indie, whom I profile in chapter 4. Then again, maybe it's something less conventional (in her third act, Annie Wilder, profiled in chapter 10, found a passion for writing a book about paranormal activity).

For some women, the word *passion* may seem too powerful. I've had a few women say to me, "I'm just not passionate about anything," or "I'm waiting till I *totally* discover a passion." But if I ask these women what interests them, they can rattle off ten things. So if you're one of those women who finds the concept of having a passion daunting, start with your interests. Take Anne's advice: "Find a little niche where you can do a little something and one thing will lead to another." The smallest step in the right direction can blossom into an incredible Act Three—think of Amy Sewell taking that ten-cents-per-word writing gig about fifth graders.

We will work on uncovering your passions in the exercises below, but first I need to explain the importance of gifts.

Finding Your Gifts

As you unearth and explore your passions, it's also important to ensure that the path you're looking at is something you can realistically do well, what I call your gifts. For most people, fulfillment requires us to both enjoy doing something (the "passion" part) and be good at doing it (the "gifted" part).

If you have a passion for painting but honestly have little talent, and this won't change no matter how much training you receive, the endeavor probably won't lead you to a satisfying third act (although it certainly can be a fun hobby). Instead, it's important to identify if you have a talent or aptitude for your passions. And don't immediately say, "I have no talent"! Many women discount their gifts, thinking *I've been home for fifteen years, I'm not good at anything anymore,* without really exploring the question. I'll show you a couple of ways to explore the question in the exercises in the next section.

So let's explore identifying something you're both good at (your gifts) and love to do (your passions)—what I call your "Gifted Passions." Once you've found your Gifted Passion, that will be something worth paying attention to.

EXERCISES FOR FINDING YOUR GIFTED PASSIONS

Fortunately, you've already gotten a head start on your Gifted Passions search in the exercises from the previous chapter. Now it's time to refine and narrow your ideas.

STEP 1: CREATE A PASSIONS LIST

Start by pulling out all the material you compiled from the dreaming big exercises in chapter 1—the "perfect day" visualization; the interviews; the thoughts you recorded while reading new publications, attending events, or exercising; and any other imagining and dreaming exercises you did. Look for those interests that seem to really jump out at you throughout several of the exercises. Hopefully, at least a few did. What themes emerged? Did you discover, for example, like one of my clients, that you are happiest when somehow engaged with dogs (reading about them, playing with them, watching TV shows about dogs), or did you realize, like another client, that you are fascinated and want to learn more about every new gadget (you like talking to techie people, you enjoy buying a new product and figuring it out).

Keeping those themes in mind, take out a piece of paper and write at the top "My Passions." For the next ten minutes, write down everything that comes into your head that you are passionate about (or if "passion" is too strong for you, that you like to do). Remember, don't discount anything because you think it's too insignificant or unworthy. Don't hesitate to add something because you think it's a cliché. You may think, *Oh, everyone likes to do this,* or *This field is too crowded,* or *Every baby boomer likes this.* Don't let that deter you. No matter what you like, be truthful about what you enjoy rather than trying to make up the thing that seems coolest or least common. If you love going to Pilates class, write it down. If you love taking walks on the beach, write it down. If you love doing research for the trips you take, write it down.

STEP 2: IDENTIFY YOUR GIFTS

Your primary gifts may not be immediately apparent to you, so it often helps to enlist a close friend to help you uncover hidden talents or aptitudes. Ask your friend to help you with this.

First, discuss with your friend the things that you do well and write them down. If you know that you sing well, that's easy—write it down. What's harder to uncover are those hidden talents, things like a talent for connecting people, a talent for solving problems, a talent for simplifying complicated tasks, a talent for spotting new clothing trends, a talent for appreciating beauty. It may take some time to think of these.

Here is one exercise that may help uncover your hidden talents. It is aimed at identifying a peak experience and the skills you used to make it successful. (*Peak experience* is a term originally coined by psychologist Abraham Maslow). Have your friend give you this prompt and write down your answers:

Tell me about a peak experience you have had in your professional or personal life. It may be a time when you felt most alive, most involved, or most excited about what you were involved in.

What made it a peak experience?

Who was involved?

What feelings did you have?

What made it so successful to you?

When I do this exercise with my clients, they relate experiences they had anywhere from a few weeks before to years earlier. I even had one client tell me about something that happened all the way back in college.

Once the interview is over, read what your friend has recorded. What talents did you use during your peak experience? Don't pigeonhole yourself—look past what you've always considered your primary strengths and abilities.

If you want an independent assessment of your natural character strengths, you can also take the Brief Strengths Test at www.authentic happiness.org, the homepage of psychologist and bestselling author Martin Seligman. The test is free, but you have to register to take it.

Finally, don't hesitate to ask other friends and family what they think your strengths are. Don't make them feel they have to say nice things about you; just tell them you're looking for a quick, honest opinion on what you seem to be good at.

STEP 3: MATCH UP YOUR GIFTS AND PASSIONS

Now it's time to score each of the passions on your list based on your talent or aptitude. So take out your Passions List from Step 1 and your Gifts list from Step 2. Assign each passion a number from 1 to 5, based on whether you feel you have a gift or talent for it. Assign a 5 if your gifts or talents will fully support this passion or any number down to 1 (1 meaning that your lack of ability does not make you a good fit for the passion).

If you really feel you have a gift for one of your passions but need additional training, you can still give it a high score if training can be obtained. For example, one of my client's passions was what she called "personal environmental sustainability"—she enjoyed limiting her individual impact on the environment and felt she had a gift for it. However, she knew that to really pursue it, she had a lot to learn: she'd need additional training to become truly proficient in things like composting and chemical-free cleaning. But she knew she could learn it. This still qualified as something she had a gift for, so we scored it a 5.

Take a look at the Passions that you rated the highest. These are your "Gifted Passions." Your Gifted Passions will be a critical part of the Power Equation, which we'll discuss in chapter 4. First, we move on to the other key component of the Power Equation: motivation.

THREE

Understanding Your Motivations

Motivation is a fire from within. If someone else tries to light that fire under you, chances are it will burn very briefly.

—Stephen R. Covey

ALL OF US ARE MOTIVATED BY different things. I may be motivated by something that holds absolutely no interest for you; you may be driven by something I never think about. In order to live the life you want, it is important to both recognize what motivates you and to figure out how to fulfill those motivations. This chapter will help you gain that understanding, and it will help you evaluate how strong that motivation is. Without strong motivation, it's hard to push yourself to do what needs to be done on the path to your third act.

How did a failing school in Chicago become radically transformed in just a few years? Through the strong motivation of stay-at-home mother Jacqueline Edelberg. She not only succeeded in transforming the school, she transformed her whole neighborhood.

JACQUELINE'S STORY

As her daughter neared preschool age, Jacqueline Edelberg was struggling with a big problem, one that many women can identify with: how to make sure her children could receive a quality education. Unfortu-

Jacqueline Edelberg

nately, the closest public school, a place called Nettelhorst, tucked into Chicago's inner-city Lakeview neighborhood, was notorious for its students' low test scores, its ramshackle condition, and its revolving door of unsuccessful principals. Jacqueline, a stay-at-home mom who was pregnant with her second child, faced an ugly dilemma. She was more likely to get her kids into Harvard than into a local alternative magnet school, and private schools were not only exclusive but also prohibitively expensive. That left her with two options: move or send her kids to Nettelhorst.

Nettelhorst was a mystery to Jacqueline and all her friends in the neighborhood. No one she knew had ever been inside. Curious, she drove to the school one day in the middle of summer with her daughter. Jacqueline pushed little Maya's stroller up to the weather-beaten front door and pulled. Locked. She pushed the stroller around the side of the building and then to the back, finding all the doors locked and the school seemingly deserted. Finally, as she rounded the last corner she spotted a security guard, who warily unlocked the front door for her.

Inside, she walked down a quiet hallway until she encountered a woman who took one look at her and began screaming: "You can't be in here! Get out! Now!" Jacqueline, unprepared for a fight, muttered that she was sorry and left.

She, however, wasn't about to give up; in fact, she was more curious than ever. Was this really a school? Or maybe, she joked with her friends, it's run by witches. She called and made an appointment for the next day. Jacqueline quickly called a friend who faced the same educational dilemma. "Nicole, you've got to come see Nettelhorst with me," she pleaded. "I really don't want to go back alone."

To their surprise, the principal of Nettelhorst welcomed them into the school and spent three hours showing them around. Besides the construction workers repairing part of the roof that had caved in, they were the only people there. As the principal flipped through a "brag book" that showcased the school's recent achievements, the moms weren't impressed. *This is not going to work*, thought Jacqueline. At the end of the meeting, the principal posed a blunt question: "What do I have to do to get your kids to come to school here?"

Jacqueline and Nicole looked at each other. "This is all very interesting, but we need to go home and think about it," said Jacqueline.

The moms headed straight back to Nicole's, parked the kids in front of *Dora the Explorer*, cracked open a bottle of wine, and started putting together a wish list for Nettelhorst. Jacqueline felt her initial curiosity about the mystery of Nettelhorst growing into true excitement. When she'd left her job as a professor to stay home with her children, she felt that down the line she'd be able to figure out a way to use the skills and education she'd acquired over the years; she just didn't realize it would be so soon. Here was a project that was unlike anything she'd ever done and that would solve a real problem for her family. As she and Nicole tried to solve the puzzle of the struggling school, they kept asking themselves, "Wait a minute, can we really do this?" They put their audacious goals in a list and prepared for their next meeting with the principal.

You can imagine that most principals might feel attacked in this situation—defensive, reluctant to help. But to Jacqueline's surprise, Nettelhorst's principal looked over the list with a brightening face.

This was what she'd been wanting. She looked up at Nicole and Jacqueline: "Let's get going, girls; it's going to be a very busy year."

Jacqueline assembled a large group of volunteers from the neighborhood—including many of her girlfriends who found themselves in the same spot she and Nicole were in—and started dividing up the tasks. Jacqueline knew that many of the neighborhood women were just like her, stay-at-home moms with an amazing breadth of talents to be harnessed. Committees were developed to look at everything from Nettelhorst's curriculum to PR efforts to encourage neighborhood kids to attend to repairing the building. Sometimes the project seemed immensely doable; at other times it seemed nearly impossible. And occasionally it even morphed into the absurd, like the time Jacqueline was spit on while painting a wall at the school by a teacher who felt threatened by the changes Jacqueline and her committee were making.

During all the work and planning there remained a nagging question. It was one thing to talk in the abstract about how great the school could be, but would Jacqueline and her friends really use their own children as the first guinea pigs and enroll them?

Finally, it was the day of the first open house, the chance to show their school off to the neighborhood. Bright murals painted by students, parents, and local artists decorated the walls, and the volunteers were excited about the work they'd done, despite their nervousness. They'd secured Rahm Emanuel to open the doors at the open house, and it was a resounding success: three hundred families attended, and seventy-eight children enrolled in Nettelhorst that day—an outcome that would've been unthinkable before Jacqueline jump-started the revival of the school.

"Working on the project changed how I viewed myself," says Jacqueline. "I kind of found my voice, and it became something of a calling. For me to have a project that was real and tangible was just the best education. I wouldn't have traded the last eight years of it for anything under the sun."

The front of Nettelhorst School after rehab

A new lunchroom at the school

Nettelhorst's transformation received widespread attention, and Jacqueline went on to write a book, *How to Walk to School*, about the experience. The school is now not only vastly improved in appearance; it's also home to arts and culture programs, an after-school kid's club, and several athletic teams. "What's funny is that I don't know anything about education, and I don't even really like children—I mean I like my own children," says Jacqueline. "It's not like I ever saw myself as a school reformer. But now I write regularly about school reform, because it seemed a shame to leave this experience as an urban myth. I want to give other reformers the tools they need to succeed. If our experience could be more than just one little urban experience, if it could bring about systemic change, that would be a remarkable thing."

Even though Jacqueline wasn't necessarily interested in education reform and didn't have a natural affinity for kids, she found a rich source of motivation that helped her pull off an intimidating project: her own vibrant curiosity, a healthy resistance to authority, and the necessity of finding a safe, enriching place to send her children to school. Reinforced by the team of headstrong women around her, she pulled Nettelhorst up from the ashes and made an impact that has resonated for years in her community.

FINDING YOUR MOTIVATION

The amount of time and energy Jacqueline Edelberg put into her volunteer work at Nettelhorst—plus the sheer amount of nerve it took—point to a woman who's highly motivated to achieve her goals. Jacqueline's primary motivation is obvious: she wanted her kids to get a good education. Imagine how the project would've gone had she not had this incentive. Sure, she'd have some motivation—the feeling of doing something positive for her community, the thrill of pushing past barriers—but it was her kids' education that impelled her to put her all into transforming the school. When times were rough, when obstacles presented themselves, Jacqueline and her partners were driven forward by the vision of the education they wanted their children to receive.

No matter what you do in your third act, you have to be motivated enough to carry it through. Nothing worthwhile comes easy, and if you don't have something constantly propelling you toward your goal, you're much less likely to get where you want to be. Here is an illustration of this principle.

Imagine that you decide to push a heavy boulder up a hill. You want to do it because you think it will look much prettier at the top of the hill. As you start to push the boulder, you feel engaged in the project and quite excited. And you push really hard to make that boulder move forward and up, inch by inch. But as soon as you stop pushing, it rolls back down the hill a little bit. Eventually you get tired and start thinking, *Why am I pushing this heavy boulder up the hill? It's harder than I thought. In fact, I really don't care whether this stupid boulder is at the top of the hill! It looks just fine right where it is.* And so you give up.

Clearly, your motivation—that the boulder would look pretty at the top of the hill—was far too weak. Your drive to reach your goal was outweighed by the difficulty of the task at hand. And when motivation is too weak, it is very easy to give up. If, instead, you were moving the boulder to the top of the hill to be rolled down upon charging armies that were about to wipe out your village, your motivation would be stronger—it would be a matter of life and death. You would use all your strength for as long as it took until you pushed the boulder to the top of the hill. Strong motivation can overcome the difficulty of almost any task.

Imagining something different for the third act of your life—and then actually accomplishing it—is not an easy task: it's the equivalent of pushing that heavy boulder up a hill. It takes hard work and constant pushing to sustain your forward momentum. But if you don't feel strongly motivated to use your Gifted Passions to achieve your third-act goal, it's quite likely you will give up when change gets difficult or uncomfortable—and it will. *Well, really, my life seems just fine as it is,* you'll tell yourself.

Here's how one woman describes being stuck with the status quo:

I feel smart, well-read, and interesting (most of the time). I think I could do anything, but I just don't know what the price will be, so I allow predictability and complacency to rule. Maybe I'm too risk-averse to start over, or maybe I will wait till when my kids are settled, perhaps married. Then I will feel free to reach for something new. Until then, I am not unhappy, just always aware that I'm sacrificing some greater potential.

See how easily we can get caught in the trap of saying, "I'll figure this out later"? We do this when our motivation is not strong enough to override our complacency.

So what kinds of motivation have that power? To keep you inspired and moving, you have to make sure your motivation is 100 percent authentic. As you identify the specific motivations that drive you, which we'll do in the exercise below, you must dig deep and look honestly at yourself. Aspiring to a motivation that you don't really have will only lead you toward failure and frustration. For example, some people are motivated very strongly to make a difference in the world. You may think, "That's a worthy motivation—I should be motivated by that, too," but in reality, you may not be. Again, in order for this exercise to be effective, you must be truthful to yourself.

The sustainability of your motivation is important, too. Many women in my survey answered that sometimes they feel the urge to change and other times they don't. We all know that feeling. When a friend gets an incredible new job, you begin to examine your own life and may feel a sudden burst of ambition, but then it wavers. If you struggle with constantly wavering levels of motivation, it's critical that you follow the steps in the second part of this book and put yourself on a set plan. When your motivation is lagging, you'll be able to use the plan to keep your forward momentum going.

EXERCISE: CREATE YOUR MOTIVATION LIST

Understanding what motivates you requires some brainstorming about why you want to make a change and then collecting the answers in a list that I call a "Motivation List." I'll start with an easy example. Say that the change you want to make is to lose twenty pounds. Your Motivation List, which would list all the reasons you are motivated to lose weight, might look like this:

I am motivated to lose twenty pounds because I want to

- *look better*
- *have more energy and not be tired*
- *correct my blood sugar problem*
- *make sure I don't have health issues in the future*
- *be as thin as my friend Jane*
- *be found sexually attractive*
- *increase my self-confidence*
- *look younger*
- *be a role model for my children*
- *improve my marriage*
- *save money on having to buy new clothes, since my old clothes don't fit anymore*

You can make a Motivation List for any change you want to make (like losing weight), but we are specifically focusing on creating change that will lead you to the life you want.

So for this Motivation List, take out a piece of paper and put at the top "I am motivated to create a different third act because I want to." Then start writing down anything that comes to mind. Be sure not to make value judgments. For example, if you realize you are motivated by wanting others to have a good opinion of you, write it down even if your inner voice is saying, *But that's so shallow, I shouldn't care about that.* And, as mentioned above, don't write that you're motivated by "making a difference in my community" just because you feel you should be motivated by that, when you really aren't. For the Motivation List to work effectively, you have to be true to yourself.

To get you started on the right path, here's a list of possible motivations for creating something great in your third act. It is in no way definitive, so add and subtract from it as you see fit. You will most likely end up with fewer than ten items on your Motivation List.

I am motivated to create a different third act because I want to

- *create a new identity*
- *generate additional income*
- *be recognized by others*
- *accomplish something new*
- *leave a legacy*
- *become more independent*
- *be more competitive*
- *achieve to my potential*
- *meet new people*
- *get out of the house more*
- *be more responsible*
- *be intellectually stimulated*
- *not waste my education and work history*
- *make a difference in the world*
- *feel better about myself/increase my self-confidence or self-worth*
- *develop new skills and talents*
- *feel productive*

- *avoid being bored*
- *serve God in some way*
- *solve problems*
- *be a role model for my children*
- *find an outlet for my creativity*
- *mentor or teach others*

If you feel comfortable sharing your motivations, ask those closest to you to confirm that they agree with your list.

Once you've arrived at the final ten or so items on your Motivation List, it's time to quantify how strong your motivation is for each item on your list. Rate each item with either a 1 or a 2, based on how strongly you want it, with 2 meaning your desire is very strong and 1 meaning your desire is there but not as strong. Now make a list of all the motivations that you rated a 2 (you probably will have around five that you rated a 2).

⌒

Now that you're down to your five strongest motivations, you are ready to complete the Power Equation, the topic of the next chapter.

FOUR

The Power Equation:
Gifted Passions Plus Motivations Lead to Powerful Results

The whole is more than the sum of its parts.

—Aristotle

THIS IS THE CHAPTER YOU'VE BEEN waiting for. Now that you've explored your Gifted Passions and your motivations, you're ready to do what I call the "Power Equation." (Don't worry, there's no math involved.) The equation is simple:

GIFTED PASSIONS + STRONG MOTIVATION = POWERFUL RESULTS

As you combine your Gifted Passions and your motivations, you'll see that the clouds will start to part. You'll be able to begin to visualize exactly what your next steps will look like.

Indie Lee's story is a perfect way to show the Power Equation in action. She'd found her Gifted Passion—organic gardening—but things really took off when the second part of the equation, motivation, fell into her lap in the most dramatic way possible. Let's take a look at how Indie's Gifted Passions and motivations added up to an incredible Act Three.

INDIE'S STORY

Indie Lee lay in the hospital awaiting surgery to remove a brain tumor. *If I wake up from this operation,* Indie thought to herself, *I have a new mission to fulfill.*

Indie Lee

Indie did wake up, and since recovering, she has been motivated to educate the world that what you put on your skin is as important as what you put in your body.

Before she'd even begun her senior year of college, Indie Lee had landed a great starter job: she had an accounting position waiting for her at the Long Island office of Ernst & Young. Being a businesswomen was something she had aspired to her whole life, ever since she began dressing up in business suits and going to the office with her father as a little girl. But when she got to Ernst & Young after completing her degree, she found herself bogged down with entry-level work.

I graduated at the top of my class, thought confident Indie. *Shouldn't I be running this operation?*

Worse, as Indie began working as an auditor, she started to feel that accounting wasn't her calling. Being the auditor felt like a necessary evil—she'd walk into a room knowing that people were thinking: *Oh goodness, the auditor's here.* She started looking at her options and mentioned to one recruiter that if there were any opportunities in the fashion or entertainment worlds, she'd be happy to hear about them. Sure enough, the recruiter called back a few weeks later with an accounting position at HBO. Indie jumped on the chance and landed the job.

Indie spent the next eight years at HBO. During that time, she got married, had two children, and did a lot of growing. But as time went on, she continued to wonder whether she really wanted to be an accountant the rest of her life and finally gave her two weeks notice. "That was petrifying," says Indie. "I think so many of us prepare our lives to get to a certain place. You go to school, you get a degree, and you get a job, and then you realize, 'Oh great, now I'm going to be an accountant my whole life.' Then how do you reinvent yourself?

"I had never in a million years thought I would stop working, and there I was, stopping working." And the reality was, Indie felt her two children needed her. Her son, Jacob, was diagnosed with dyslexia, and her daughter, Emily, was just three at the time.

Just taking care of the children didn't seem like enough, so Indie thought about what she loved to do. She realized she had always loved gardening as a child, so she built a 750-square-foot greenhouse in her backyard, which became her new office. She started growing all sorts of vegetables and edible flowers, and as she spent more time with her plants, her conception of herself began to shift. She was no longer that corporate accounting person she'd been for so many years. But she was still driven to succeed, and she began looking at ways to make her love of gardening her second career.

Indie has a philosophy that when one door closes another will open. One day while shopping at Whole Foods she said to an employee, "Hey, I see you have a farmers' market. I have a greenhouse, and I grow certified-organic vegetables and starter plants. Is that something you'd be interested in?" Soon Whole Foods was calling her for edible flowers. She also talked to local restaurateurs, and within a few months she was delivering wheatgrass, sprouts, and salad greens—all organic—to restaurants around town.

Indie had found her Gifted Passion. It was then time for a powerful motivation to drop into her lap and push her third act into overdrive.

As Indie's plants flourished, her sister prepared to give birth to her first child. Once while Indie and her very pregnant sister were shopping for baby things, Indie read, for the first time, the label on a bottle of baby lotion. She was stunned by the toxicity of the ingredients. "No, no, no," she said to her sister. "This stuff is *not* going on my little nephew's brand-new butt. He has no immune system yet!" As soon as she got home, she began experimenting with making powders out of arrowroot, cornstarch, pure organic essential oils, and flowers and lavender that she cut from the garden. Her natural baby powder would be a great gift for the upcoming baby shower.

At the same time, Indie was experiencing some unsettling health problems. She'd dealt with rheumatoid arthritis for years, and she had begun noticing weakness in her peripheral vision along with a few intense headaches. Something just didn't feel right. She went for an MRI, and when the doctor called later the same day, she knew it wouldn't be good news. "I have a brain tumor, don't I?" she said before he could speak.

"Wait," he replied. "Come on down and we can talk about it."

"No, I need to know before I make the drive," Indie said insistently.

After a short pause, the doctor said, "Yes, you have something up there."

"I'll be there in fifteen minutes," said Indie.

On the drive to the doctor's office, Indie was terrified, but something told her that it wasn't the end. Over the following weeks, she visited some of the best specialists in the county. When she asked how this could've happened to her—a relatively healthy woman—the doctors replied that it could've been something environmental.

It was an "aha" moment for Indie. She had a flashback to shopping with her sister and thinking about all the toxins we put on our skin—our largest organ. As Indie waited for her surgery, she redoubled her efforts in making natural, safe, baby-care products, pulling from her passion for nature and her new motivation to keep her nephew from encountering the harmful substances that could've contributed to her tumor.

At the baby shower, she presented her new products to her sister and explained to all the guests how they were made with all-natural essential oils. She explained how she'd achieved a pleasant smell that wasn't overpowering or synthetic. She explained what "all natural" means and why she chose the ingredients. She explained how she'd made baby oils and massage oils because circulation is so important for the baby. She explained the benefit of the calendula flowers she'd put into her diaper rash balm.

Everyone in the room was fascinated. They all wanted Indie's products. *This is what I have to do,* Indie told herself, and she got to work on a full baby line. The endeavor distracted her from thoughts of the tumor that was growing in her brain. Working on the new products— talking to specialists and doing extensive research—consumed Indie until the day of her surgery and helped her keep a positive outlook.

Indie in her greenhouse

"Of course I was scared, and there were definitely days that I cried. What was important was to live every day to the fullest. So often we go through life and we 'just go through it'; we don't actually play it out and live.

"There's that saying, 'Don't sweat the small stuff, and it's all small stuff.' After a tumor, it's all small stuff. I mean, really, how much worse could it get? I can remember saying good-bye to my children

Indie on the beach with her daughter

before surgery, wondering if I was going to be there again. That to this day brings tears to my eyes. There's nothing worse than that."

Then, on April 22, 2009, she awoke from surgery. It was Earth Day. "Welcome to the rest of your life," said the doctor. "Congratulations. You're done." From that day, Indie saw things with a new clarity, and she has only seen her motivation to create safe, natural skin-care products grow. Her line of products, called Indie Lee, has grown into a full set of balms, scrubs, shampoos, moisturizers, and cleansers for adults and babies. "I know that the product line will continue to develop and be super successful," says Indie. "There's no doubt in my mind. But my real motivation is to bring this awareness to more and more people, that what you put on your skin is as important as what you put in your body.

"When I look back, it's clear that how I started is not at all where I ended up. But it's the journey that's the fun part. I stopped trying to figure out where I have to be, what it has to look like, exactly the route it has to take, and just let it happen naturally."

DOING THE POWER EQUATION

When you combine your Gifted Passions and your motivations from your Motivation List, the whole that comes into view can be quite startling. When Indie built her greenhouse, she had no idea she'd also be building an organic skin-care line from scratch a few years later. But that's where the combination of a Gifted Passion and a strong motivation took her.

The Power Equation looks simple—and indeed it is—but using it to get to a real breakthrough takes some work. I promise it's worth it. Take out several blank sheets of paper and follow these steps:

STEP 1. Revisit the exercises at the end of chapters 2 and 3, and list your top five Gifted Passions and top five motivations in two side-by-side columns.

GIFTED PASSIONS	MOTIVATIONS
1.	1.
2.	2.
3.	3.
4.	4.
5.	5.

STEP 2. Start with the first Gifted Passion on your list. Match it up with the first motivation, and think about whether there's an outcome or a path that seems to grow naturally from the combination. Then take the same Gifted Passion and try matching it up with the second motivation on the list, repeating until you've run through all five motivations.

This may sound a little confusing, so let me use myself as an example. If I were doing the Power Equation, one of my Gifted Passions would be dancing. My top five motivations are:

1. *to acquire new skills*

2. *to gain recognition*

3. *to mentor others*

4. *to make a difference*

5. *to be creative*

So here's what my Power Equation for my Gifted Passion of dance would look like:

GIFTED PASSION FOR DANCING +
MOTIVATION TO ACQUIRE SKILLS =

- ○ *Master new forms of dancing; focus on technical improvement*

GIFTED PASSION FOR DANCING +
MOTIVATION TO GAIN RECOGNITION =

- ○ *Become a performer*

GIFTED PASSION FOR DANCING +
MOTIVATION TO MENTOR OTHERS =

- ○ *Start a dance school; give private dance lessons; speak about how dance can be a part of education*

GIFTED PASSION FOR DANCING +
MOTIVATION TO MAKE A DIFFERENCE =

- ○ *Raise money for dance scholarships; organize a dance benefit for a cause I believe in*

GIFTED PASSION FOR DANCING +
MOTIVATION TO BE CREATIVE =

- ○ *Find opportunities to choreograph*

STEP 3. After you complete the exercise in Step 2 with the first Gifted Passion, repeat the entire exercise with each of the next four. If you're struggling to get through all the combinations, look for ways to make it fun. Set aside an afternoon and work on the exercise at your favorite coffee shop or a neighborhood park. Or ask a good friend or your spouse to do the exercise with you. Trust me, even if you're already familiar with the passions and motivations you've put on your list, the results of fusing them in new ways can be amazing. The picture you arrive at is often far more than the sum of its parts.

Barbara's Power Equation

One of my clients, Barbara, completed this exercise as homework prior to a coaching session. During our session, she started to cry as she told me how she felt when she completed her Power Equation. The answer to what she should be doing had jumped out at her. "It had been right there all along, but I would never have discovered it," she told me, wiping away tears of relief.

Here is Barbara's Power Equation exercise in full, with her five Gifted Passions. You'll see that Barbara filled in the right side of her equations with both vocational titles ("designer") and activities ("taking art classes"). At this point, you're just getting ideas down, and they can be either short-term endeavors or committed paths, so feel free to do the same as you write out your Power Equations.

1. GIFTED PASSION FOR PROBLEM SOLVING + MOTIVATION TO BE CREATIVE =

- *advertising art director*
- *designer*
- *interior decorator*
- *space planner (floor planning)*
- *visualizing how a remodel could look by creating 3-D sketches*
- *staging*
- *custom home refinements*
- *Web design*

2. GIFTED PASSION FOR PROBLEM SOLVING + MOTIVATION TO HAVE NEW EXPERIENCES =

- *researcher*
- *quality-assurance tester*
- *book editor/proofreader*
- *writer (magazine articles, children's books)*

**3. GIFTED PASSION FOR PROBLEM SOLVING +
MOTIVATION TO BE SOCIAL =**

- ○ *member of think tank*
- ○ *group brainstorming*

**4. GIFTED PASSION FOR PROBLEM SOLVING +
MOTIVATION TO BE RECOGNIZED =**

- ○ *troubleshooter/consultant in the business world*

**5. GIFTED PASSION FOR RESEARCH +
MOTIVATION TO BE CREATIVE =**

- ○ *genealogy research*
- ○ *personal shopper*
- ○ *product research for* Real Simple *magazine
  or* Consumer Reports

**6. GIFTED PASSION FOR RESEARCH +
MOTIVATION TO HAVE NEW EXPERIENCES/INTELLECTUAL
STIMULATION/LIFELONG LEARNING =**

- ○ *consultant/personal shopper for recently divorced
  male executives as they decorate and furnish their new home*
- ○ *consultant/personal shopper for single or divorced women
  buying a new car*
- ○ *downsizing consultant*
- ○ *relocation consultant working with real estate company or
  relocation company (provide community information)*
- ○ *event planner*

7. GIFTED PASSION FOR RESEARCH +
MOTIVATION TO BE SOCIAL =

- *vocational counselor*
- *vacation planner/travel agent*
- *Club Med salesperson*

8. GIFTED PASSION FOR RESEARCH +
MOTIVATION TO HAVE A SENSE OF ACCOMPLISHMENT/CLOSURE =

- *personal concierge*

9. GIFTED PASSION FOR RESEARCH +
MOTIVATION TO BE RECOGNIZED =

- *personal concierge*

10. GIFTED PASSION FOR CREATING ART +
MOTIVATION TO BE CREATIVE =

- *successful artist*

11. GIFTED PASSION FOR CREATING ART +
MOTIVATION TO HAVE NEW EXPERIENCES =

- *working in new art mediums*
- *jewelry making*
- *taking art classes*
- *creating art on location in new places*
- *traveling artist*
- *participating in paint-outs in various cities*

12. GIFTED PASSION FOR CREATING ART +
MOTIVATION TO BE SOCIAL =

- *art teacher*
- *workshop leader/participant*
- *creating custom art for someone's hobby or passion*
- *art teacher for kids/people with behavioral issues (art therapy)*

13. GIFTED PASSION FOR CREATING ART +
MOTIVATION TO HAVE A SENSE OF ACCOMPLISHMENT/CLOSURE =

- *selling art through Internet, galleries, stores, art shows, or on the street*
- *being part of a gallery show*

14. GIFTED PASSION FOR CREATING ART +
MOTIVATION TO BE RECOGNIZED =

- *fine artist/professional artist*
- *children's book illustrator*
- *having my poetry published*
- *writing articles for magazines*

15. GIFTED PASSION FOR EXPLORING NEW DESTINATIONS/CITIES +
MOTIVATION TO BE CREATIVE =

- *travel consultant*
- *writer/reviewer of a region's food/wine event*
- *teach art workshops on location*
- *coordinating art shows*
- *create location/stock photography*

**16. GIFTED PASSION FOR EXPLORING NEW DESTINATIONS/CITIES +
MOTIVATION TO DO RESEARCH =**

- *tour guide*

**17. GIFTED PASSION FOR EXPLORING NEW DESTINATIONS/CITIES +
MOTIVATION TO BE SOCIAL =**

- *tour guide: specialize in female-oriented events
  or a specific club's events like a girl's trip to Provence,
  a gardener's group tour of specialty regional gardens,
  a shopping trip to Longenberger/Vera Bradley/Amish country*

**18. GIFTED PASSION FOR EXPLORING NEW DESTINATIONS/CITIES +
MOTIVATION TO HAVE A SENSE OF ACCOMPLISHMENT =**

- *traveling art teacher*
- *travel to a school each quarter, taking students off-site in warm
  weather and to museums in winter*

**19. GIFTED PASSION FOR EXPLORING NEW DESTINATIONS/CITIES +
MOTIVATION TO BE RECOGNIZED =**

- *partcipant in outdoor art shows*
- *art critic (review gallery openings)*

**20. GIFTED PASSION FOR MAKING THINGS BEAUTIFUL +
MOTIVATION TO BE CREATIVE =**

- *creating painted furniture*
- *landscape design*
- *create recycled functional art (e.g., turning a used piece
  of furniture into a custom-painted reupholstered piece)*
- *painting interior murals (kids' rooms)*
- *floral arranger*

21. GIFTED PASSION FOR MAKING THINGS BEAUTIFUL + MOTIVATION TO HAVE NEW EXPERIENCES =

- *interior decorator*
- *sidewalk chalk artist*

22. GIFTED PASSION FOR MAKING THINGS BEAUTIFUL + MOTIVATION TO BE SOCIAL =

- *teaching craft workshops*
- *working at Pottery Barn*
- *makeup artist*

23. GIFTED PASSION FOR MAKING THINGS BEAUTIFUL + MOTIVATION TO HAVE A SENSE OF ACCOMPLISHMENT =

- *city cleanup artist (murals)*

After you complete your Power Equation exercise, put it away. After a week has passed, pull it out and read back through all the possibilities that your Gifted Passions and motivations opened up. Do any of your ideas give you the feeling Barbara had, that the answer has been there all along? By the way, Barbara chose her last answer in number 12: "art therapy." She is currently enrolled in a masters program for art therapists. I often find that one or two things really jump out as my clients scan what they've written. If you do latch onto something promising, congratulations—we'll be looking more closely at how you can get started with it in the remainder of the book.

But if it didn't happen, that's fine too. Simply pick a few possibilities that make the most sense right now. As we'll see again and again, your plans don't have to be perfect. You don't have to see clouds parting and hear angelic strains of music. As Indie says, "Get an idea and stop thinking. Just do it."

I hope you're excited by all the possibilities you dug up by completing your Power Equation. In the next chapter, we'll be exploring the power of visualizing success. Hopefully you have a couple of Power Equation results to start visualizing with. In chapter 1, we talked about visualizing as a way of opening up possibilities for your future; in the next chapter, we'll be talking about something more specific. I'll show you how a powerful vision can drive your Act Three and sustain you through times of uncertainty.

FIVE

Visualizing Success

Far away there in the sunshine are my highest aspirations.
I may not reach them, but I can look up and see their beauty,
believe in them, and try to follow where they lead.

—*Louisa May Alcott*

PERHAPS YOU HAVE HEARD THE JOKE about the little old man, Harvey, who really wants to win the lottery. Each day he gets down on his knees and prays, "Dear God, please let today be the day that I win." This goes on for several years, but he never wins. Finally, one day when the little old man is down on his knees praying yet again, he hears the voice of God: "Harvey, meet me halfway. Buy a lottery ticket."

I love this story because it's so accurately portrays the challenge that many of us have in moving from thought to action. We can think and wish and pray that we're going to win the lottery or start a business or help foster children or do anything else, but if we don't move—if we don't at least buy the lottery ticket—nothing happens.

So in these next several chapters, you will learn how to take your imagined idea to action. You start by (1) taking the one idea from the first section of the book that has the most appeal and (2) asking yourself, "If I did that, what would success look like?" This vision of success will be the beacon of light that you will strive to reach.

Terry Grahl had a dramatic vision that inspired her to embark on a third act in which she put her interior design skills to work in a whole new way. Her story goes to show that your vision needn't be dramatic—hers started with a polka-dotted pillow. Yet it grew to be powerful enough that Terry now brings joy into the lives of homeless women and children across the country.

TERRY'S STORY

Terry Grahl was an award-winning interior designer living in a town on the outskirts of Detroit with her husband and four kids—three boys, one girl. One cold December day her phone rang. It was the event coordinator for a local women's shelter; he wanted to know if Terry would be able to help redecorate the shelter. "We would be so grateful even if you just painted one wall," he said.

Terry quickly agreed, even though she was a little fearful, having never been inside a shelter. "I went in there thinking that I'd be Ms. Superhero, make a difference, paint my one wall, and go home," she remembers. It didn't exactly work out that way. When Terry stepped into the shelter, she was overcome with memories of her own hard-scrabble childhood, of her family losing their home and descending into poverty. She remembered the food stamps, the Christmases with no presents under the tree, the homemade clothes. She'd blocked out these memories for years, but as she looked around the shelter, taking in the stained floors, drooping ceiling lights, and wood paneling held to the wall with duct tape, the memories came flooding back with a vengeance. She took several pictures of the shelter and returned home.

Terry as a child

For the next week, sadness lingered with Terry. She couldn't shake the thought of women living in the place she'd visited. As she sat at her computer a few days later reviewing the photos she'd taken, one image struck her with particular force. It was a picture of one of the bunk beds, pushed up against an unfinished Sheetrock wall. Lying on the bare, stained mattress, was one case-less pillow that had a light, white-on-white polka-dot pattern. Her mind transformed that ugly image into something very different: she saw a pretty, feminine, polka-dotted pillow, trimmed with a big flowing ruffle.

As she allowed the vision to expand, she saw a bright, cheerful room. She heard the laughs of the women and the giggles of the children. She saw the sunlight spreading across the tidy floors, the freshly painted walls, and the welcoming beds. Each night before bed, she returned to this vision and drew strength from it. "That polka-dotted pillow changed my life and my journey," Terry often tells people.

Terry in the shelter before the makeover

She returned to the shelter with plans to do much more than paint a wall. She'd drawn up a plan to redesign and totally transform the place. The coordinator was excited. Terry just needed to raise the funds—an area in which she had no experience.

At first, nothing went right. Terry struggled to convey her vision for the shelter to others while balancing her family's needs. She was sending out mass e-mail to everyone she knew and not getting any response. At last her first donation came, from Australia. Once that happened, she promised herself she wouldn't quit.

She crafted a new email, this time asking for donations of mattresses, mattress pads, and pillows to furnish the fifteen bunk beds in the shelter. A week after the email went out, she sat up in bed. It was the morning of April 16, her birthday. Before her feet touched the floor, she made a request to God. "I don't want anything for my birthday except for one thing: a big donation." Before noon, she got a call from the owner of a mattress store. He was on vacation in Mexico but called her as soon as he heard about her need and agreed to donate all the mattresses, pads, and pillows. "To get that call from Mexico was just . . . *wow!*" says Terry.

Visualization of the completed shelter continued to drive her forward in the project. "I knew what the end should look like, and I worked back from there," says Terry. "Every night when I went to bed, in my mind I saw the dorm done. I saw the women smiling. I could feel what they were feeling."

Six months later, the renewed shelter was complete. Terry had felt a new part of herself awaken: "I had found my true calling. I wanted to use all of my talents and skills to provide refuge, solace, and hope to women and children in the shelters." She also discovered skills she didn't know she had: organizing, and leading enthusiastic volunteers and donors nationwide to help her carry out her vision as she began to take on additional volunteer projects at other shelters across the country.

During this time, Terry was also doing some design work for private clients. But every time the phone rang, she found herself hoping that it was a donor, not a private client, calling.

Two years after she'd received the initial call for help from the shelter, Terry sat with her mother, explaining her dilemma. She was thinking about closing her business to focus solely on her volunteer work, but her family needed the income from her private client projects. After listening to her daughter present the problem, Terry's mother said, "I'm not going to discuss this anymore. You know where God needs you to be. You need to do it." Terry drove home, her mind racing. When she got to her bedroom, she was bawling. She was lost and scared. But in that moment, she told God she was going to do this thing.

It was time for a new vision, much bigger than what she'd had for the first shelter. She saw her new organization, Enchanted Makeovers growing to national recognition—to the Susan G. Komen level. She saw her team helping shelters around the world. She envisioned a national TV show that showcased their work, inspiring viewers to think about what they wanted to do with their own lives.

With that grand vision firmly implanted in her mind, it was time for Terry to think about all the steps needed to get there and then to start focusing on what needed to happen now. "If you don't focus on *now*, that vision isn't going to happen," she says.

Five years later, Terry and her all-volunteer team have done incredible work throughout the country. They've bettered the lives of

Terry in a women's shelter rehabbed by Enchanted Makeovers

countless women and children, giving them safe, beautiful places to stay when they fall on hard times. They focus on handmade products that are donated to the cause, believing that the creators weave love and positive energy into the products they make.

Building Enchanted Makeovers has taken a lot of faith. At a recent event at a shelter in New Jersey, they had everything lined up, with more than fifty volunteers from all over the United States—makeup artists, hairdressers, manicurists, and photographers. One small thing stood in the way: Terry had no funds to get there from Michigan. "I'm getting nervous about you not getting there," one of her board members said. "I'm not," Terry replied. "It'll happen." Two days before she was to leave for New Jersey, Enchanted Makeovers received a check from J. C. Penney for the exact amount needed to cover Terry's flights and hotel stay.

"I always put the cart before the horse," says Terry. "That's how I live. I visualize the ending, the beautiful shelter makeover or growing the organization to Komen level and then just jump in and start writing the chapter. The middle will take care of itself."

LEARNING TO VISUALIZE SUCCESS

In his book *Man's Search for Meaning*, Viktor Frankl describes living in a World War II concentration camp under the most deplorable' conditions. Frankl, who before his internment had been a respected psychiatrist, understood that his survival depended on being able to visualize a better future. So he forced himself to see the future he desired: "I saw myself standing on the platform of a well-lit, warm, and pleasant lecture room. In front of me sat an attentive audience on comfortable upholstered seats. I was giving a lecture on the psychology of the concentration camp." Through this visualization of a successful future, Frankl survived his ordeal and went on to inspire millions with his story.

What does a story from a concentration camp have to do with you? While survival is not at stake, the concept of visualizing success is still relevant to anyone who wants to change. If you can't decide what success looks like to you, how can you plan how to get there, or even know when you've reached it?

To begin visualizing your own success, ask yourself, "What will it look like when I get there?" In my case, when I launched Act Three, I thought about what would be the ultimate measure of my success, and I could clearly see the answer. The ultimate level of success for me, the one thing that would tell me I had achieved what I had hoped for, was to be interviewed by Oprah. I had a vision of sitting on Oprah's couch, explaining to her how I had helped thousands of women discover their Act Three. Can't you just picture that? Now we all know that's not going to happen, but who cares. It was and still is a great motivator to me.

And without that vision, I wouldn't know what I was shooting for. Whenever I have a new idea to pursue, I think, *Will this take me one step closer to Oprah's couch?* (I call this the "Oprah Question.") If the answer is yes, I go for it. This book is one example. When I asked myself the Oprah Question as to whether I should spend the considerable time it would take to write a book, the answer was quite clear. Of course a book would move me closer to her couch, and so here it is.

Julie writing the book with her dog, Joey

WHAT DOES SUCCESS LOOK LIKE TO YOU?

The first step is to create your vision of success. In the previous chapters, you have imagined clearly what you want to do next. Take that idea and think about what the ultimate measure of success will be if you achieve what you have imagined. What is your vision of success, and what's the Oprah Question that you will use to decide whether something will get you closer to it? Sometimes women are afraid that they will visualize the wrong thing or that they will visualize too grandly. Here is a critical piece of information: you can't be wrong or too grand, because *it doesn't matter one bit whether the future you visualize is truly where you end up*. Actually, it most likely won't be where you end up. What matters is shooting for the goal because it will lead you somewhere interesting. Remember how Indie started with a greenhouse in her backyard to grow wheatgrass? That's not at all what she is doing today. As Indie says, "Just have a picture in your mind of what you'd like, and go after it. When I look back, it's clear that how I started is not at all where I ended up." Had Indie not visualized herself as an organic farmer with her greenhouse and started down that path, she wouldn't have an organic skin-care line today.

So what is your ultimate measure of success if you achieve what you have imagined? Let's say you have imagined improving the quality of music education in the public schools. Perhaps your grand vision would be an image of the stage at Carnegie Hall filled with young musicians you have gathered from around the country. Or perhaps you have imagined designing and selling your own stylish hats, and your grand vision is a picture of Julia Roberts wearing one of your creations or your hat winning a prize for best new product awarded by *Inc.* magazine.

The idea of what success looks like may just pop into your head, or it may take some time to figure it out. Take the time to get that vision and really flesh it out. It's worth it. Once you've got it, it's even fun to create an image to look at to help you when your motivation flags. I have a picture of Oprah sitting on her couch on the wall above my desk. She stares at me every day, egging me on.

⨍

Looking back at the vision you came up with, you may find yourself wondering whether you have what it takes. Sure, you have an interest, a related skill, and a motivation—but can you really pull it off?

That question strikes fear into the hearts of so many women, especially as they take stock of their lives at forty, fifty, sixty years of age. Fortunately, there's a great antidote to the fear and uncertainty: action. Action is the antidote to fear, as you will learn in the remainder of the book.

By now, you have an idea of your Gifted Passions, your motivations, and the vision that will push you on. That's great—you're building an important foundation for your third act. But as I mentioned in the introduction, I emphasize with every one of my clients that the "doing" part is just as important as the "imagining." So now that I've got you thinking about all the incredible things you're capable of, let's move on to the action.

The remaining chapters of this book will focus on the "doing" part and the issues you're likely to encounter as you begin creating the life you want. To start, let's take a look at how to start making the little changes that empower us to tackle our third-act goals. It's a process I call "getting in Change Shape."

SIX

Getting in Change Shape

*I had to pick myself up and get on with it,
do it all over again, only even better this time.*

—*Sam Walton*

I LIKE TO THINK OF HOW uncomfortable a snake must feel when it first sheds its skin and lies exposed, and yet it is just that uneasy transition that is necessary in order for the snake to transform and grow. Change is just like that for humans too. It's uncomfortable while we go through it, but it's also necessary for us to grow. And there are plenty of uncomfortable changes that happen when a woman begins searching for her third act and then goes through the process of actually getting there. That's why I recommend getting used to handling change. I call this process "getting in Change Shape™."

Mary Beth Knight was a chain-smoking, seriously overweight, unhappily married wife who one day decided it was time to stop waiting for the world to facilitate her happiness. Mary Beth set out to get in shape, one step at a time. Though an unlikely candidate for a fitness guru, that's what she became. But she wasn't just training her body. Mary Beth's story illustrates just how important it is to build our capability to embrace and thrive on change.

MARY BETH'S STORY

After several years in an abusive marriage, Mary Beth Knight decided it was time to start over. She left her husband and moved back to her hometown of Cincinnati. But she was sixty pounds overweight and smoking nearly a pack a day—hardly an auspicious condition for starting a new life. Yet she was tired of playing the victim and feeling she was just muddling through.

Mary Beth before

After living for some time in Cincinnati, she realized that the world wasn't going to facilitate her happiness. *It's my life, and I'm going to take it back,* she told herself.

Dropping the smoking habit was the first change she had to make. Mary Beth decided to do what she saw as the opposite of smoking: exercise. At the urging of a friend, she joined a gym called Revolution and started running. "I felt like Forrest Gump. I was just kind of running from life," says Mary Beth. "I was running from fear and from pain and from disappointment." When she started, she couldn't even run a mile, but she pressed on, knowing that she was training her body and mind for even further change.

Before she knew it, Mary Beth had signed up for her first race. As she walked toward the starting line, she couldn't hold back tears of fear. Her father, there to cheer her on, took hold of her arm, stopping her in her tracks. "You know, most people don't have the courage to sign up," he said. "You haven't even taken a step, but you've already won." With those words of encouragement, she took off. But toward the end of the run, she wanted to quit. The course swam in front of her, and every muscle in her body screamed for rest. She wanted to lie down, even though the pavement was steaming hot. But then she heard the announcer's voice shouting out people's names at the finish line, and an intense desire to hear her own name overtook her. Strengthened, she took step after step until she heard her own name called over the loudspeaker.

Mary Beth finishing an Ironman Triathlon

"It was probably the most freeing moment of my life," says Mary Beth. "I thought, I can actually accomplish something. I can actually set a goal, work hard for it, and make it happen. That was probably the first time I had done that. It wasn't just that I could physically cross the finish line; it was that my brain started to allow for different possibilities in life to happen."

Mary Beth was not only making important strides toward physical health; she was also getting in Change Shape mentally. She was learning how to prepare herself for transformation by pushing herself into uncomfortable places little by little.

Mary Beth continued her personal transformation, becoming a personal trainer and Spinning instructor at Revolution, and developing a close friendship with Barb, the gym's owner. The next big change in Mary Beth's life came when Barb took Mary Beth out for coffee and announced that her family had decided to relocate to Utah. She would be closing down Revolution—unless Mary Beth wanted to buy it and take it over. "Nobody else understands the spirit of the gym," explained Barb.

Mary Beth was saddened by the news that her best friend was moving, but at the same time she felt an exhilarating rush. "Of course," she blurted out before she could stop herself. Revolution had become too important to her to give up.

Because she had been working to get in Change Shape—she'd strengthened her change muscles over the previous two years by pushing herself out of her old lifestyle—she felt somewhat confident taking over management of the gym, but she was also really scared. Sometimes she still felt like the person whom people had nicknamed "Thunder Thighs" and "Mary Butt" as a kid. "I didn't feel like I knew enough. I mean, I'd been hanging out at the gym for two years, and then, suddenly, I was supposed to run it. Somehow, I just trusted that I would learn what I needed to."

Over the next few years, Mary Beth's fitness career flourished. She found incredible fulfillment seeing her clients shed pounds and develop confidence at Revolution. From the start, the gym had focused not just on the physical side of things; it also helped members

Mary Beth training at her gym, Revolution

develop new lifestyles and handle emotional impediments, much the way Mary Beth herself had learned. She had become able to take on new, exciting challenges even as she helped her clients get in Change Shape themselves.

By now, Mary Beth had remarried and had two kids, both of whom were born via C-section. She found herself asking the questions that so many mothers ask after a C-section: How do I recover from this surgery? Will I ever be comfortable with my midsection again? Mary Beth, always up for a new challenge, started thinking. *Other body parts can be repaired. Why not this?*

She went to her doctor and said, "I'm going to write a book about this." She started talking to experts and moms. She even stood in the operating room and watched a couple of C-sections take place. The result was *Strategies for the C-Section Mom*, a holistic health and well-being guide that prepares moms for C-sections and helps them recover and regain fitness afterward. "I wanted to write a book that would help ease women's minds about the surgery and then give them a strategy," says Mary Beth. "I feel that if we have a plan, we have knowledge, and we have power. Then it's just putting one foot in front of the other."

Fifteen years after she first walked through the doors of Revolution, Mary Beth has become one of those people who hardly recognizes pictures of her old self. No longer scared and dependent, she's become a healthy, self-confident woman who thrives on change. She's developed many successful fitness products, including the mommy-muscle program and the StrollerFit franchise system. She's served as a spokesperson for Aveeno. She's contributed to *Babytalk*, *Fit Pregnancy*, and *Parenting* magazines as a pre- and postnatal fitness expert. In addition to working side by side with her husband, Eric, at Revolution every day, she records weekly fitness segments for local TV stations and serves as Cincinnati's "go-to girl" for everything health and well-being related, through her blog and frequent speaking appearances.

Even with all this success, Mary Beth is actually proud that she fails every day at something. "If I don't fail at something every day, I didn't try to really challenge myself. And if you don't challenge yourself, you're never going to surprise yourself."

GETTING IN CHANGE SHAPE

Setting off in a new direction for your third act requires a major life change—and major change is rarely comfortable. Think of the last time you went through a big life adjustment. Perhaps you moved to a new city or volunteered for a big community project. Maybe your husband lost his job, or your youngest child left for college. Whether the change was positive or negative, expected or unexpected, there was almost certainly a period of anxiety and unease as you defined your new role.

Whether we seek it (as you are doing in building a plan for Act Three) or it seeks us (the death of a parent, the loss of a job), change is coming our way. Why then, don't we prepare ourselves to handle change? Obviously, it's impossible to predict the precise changes you'll have to deal with in life, which is why I encourage women to get in Change Shape. When you're regularly exercising the muscles it takes to adapt and grow, you can be ready to handle almost anything.

Handling major change with grace and ease is kind of like becoming a runner, like Mary Beth. Would you just wake up one day and say, "I think I'll run 26.2 miles today"? Of course not. You would start training for the marathon months in advance, starting with shorter distances and gradually getting in shape. Each week you would feel stronger and better able to tackle the big race. When you'd hit a bump in the road—maybe you'd pull a hamstring—you'd figure out a plan to deal with the injury and move on.

Getting ready for your third act is a lot like that. You have to be in shape. And the best training regimen, just as with running, starts with those shorter distances, or in this case small challenges. Constantly tackling small challenges that take you out of your comfort zone builds the muscle (or capacity) for handling the big race or the major change.

Sue is an example of someone who jumped right into her third act without first getting in shape. "Basically, I went from a stay-at-home mom, with no major responsibilities other than making sure the kids got where they needed to go and dinner was on the table, to working in a stressful, fast-paced office. I was trying to adjust to my new life and at the same time learn all the new technology and ways of doing business. The amount of change was just overwhelming, and I couldn't keep up. I quit after four months."

To avoid what happened to Sue, I actually practice getting in—and staying in—Change Shape. In the last six months, here are a few of my small challenges: I took an online writing class with writers from the *New York Times*; I took a seminar on Genesis from a religious expert whom I admired; I took a ballet class with the professional dancers of Cincinnati Ballet (this one really scared me, as a fifty-two-year-old standing at the barre next to all these skinny, pretty twentysome-things); I spent a day working with a speech coach to hone my speaking skills; I interviewed women for my book (something I had never done before); and I ran in a 10K race (pushing past my typical three-mile run). Each small challenge scared me in a different way, and each time I succeeded with these little challenges, I built up my confidence and got in a little better shape to tackle big changes that I seek or that get thrown my way.

Julie running a 10K

FIVE RULES FOR GETTING IN CHANGE SHAPE

For this to work optimally, there are five rules to follow:

1. Choose smaller challenges at first, those that have a good chance of success. This builds confidence, and confidence is one of the key muscles needed to tackle major change.

2. Pick things that push you a little or scare you a little or that require learning something new. You have to get slightly out of your comfort zone, without biting off too much. If you love giving dinner parties and know you excel at it, then giving a dinner party isn't really going to push you. So if you want to pick the dinner party as one of your challenges, you would need to choose a recipe that is daunting and that might fail, or choose to throw a party for twenty guests when the most you have cooked for is ten.

3. If you fail at one of your challenges—let's say you don't complete a project you volunteered for—treat it as a pulled hamstring, not an amputated leg. Learn to accept the failure. (Remember Mary Beth's words: "I fail every day.") Don't dwell on the failure. Figure out what went wrong and why, then move on to the next challenge.

4. Mix up the challenges so that they are sometimes physical and sometimes cerebral. For example, follow up a challenge to walk to the grocery store instead of driving with a challenge to read and discuss a dense, important book.

5. Plan your challenges in advance so you know they are coming and can prepare for each one. Get out your calendar and look at the next six months. Plan to tackle a small challenge about every two weeks; I've found that once every two weeks is a good middle ground between "too much" and "not enough." If you try too many challenges too often, you can develop what I call "change fatigue." You become overwhelmed and tired—think of all those sore muscles and achy joints when you have worked out too hard. But, with too few challenges, attempted too infrequently, you never push yourself enough to get in the best Change Shape. You become the runner who thinks she's ready for the marathon after working up to 5 miles.

Once you've started the process of getting in Change Shape, you'll be able to take on bigger and bigger challenges. But it's important to not obsess over being completely ready for every initiative you take on. Sometimes you have to just jump in—you have to follow an impulse, take action, and educate yourself as you go along. This is a process called "Launching and Learning," and you can use it to great effect in your Act Three.

SEVEN

Launching and Learning

The man who removes a mountain
begins by carrying away small stones.

—*William Faulkner*

IN CHAPTER 5 YOU CREATED YOUR vision for what success looks like, your equivalent of my Oprah picture. In this chapter you will begin the process of moving toward that vision. For many women, beginning that process of moving toward the vision is really challenging. They think, *But I don't know how to do this,* or *I don't know whether I will be any good at it.* And as quick as that, a good—maybe even great—idea gets stopped dead in its tracks. So what's the best way to overcome these feelings?

My answer is to set out to achieve something without worrying about knowing everything beforehand—to Launch and then Learn.

Marion Luna Brem has done just that. She was a single mom living in Dallas; recovering from breast and cervical cancer at age thirty, she faced half a million dollars in medical bills. Needing a job desperately, but not really knowing what she would be good at, she thought, *Why not car sales?* She had to fight her way into the male-dominated industry tooth and nail, but Marion was soon one of the city's top sellers. By age thirty-six, she owned her own car dealership and today runs one of the largest women-owned businesses in all of Texas.

MARION'S STORY

Marion as a child

Eleven-year-old Marion Luna walked through her empty living room, trailed by her classmate, Kate, who stopped and looked around at the bare floor and walls. "Where's the furniture?"

"Oh . . . it's still being shipped from our old house. It's on its way," Marion lied.

The furniture wasn't on its way. In reality, her family just moved so much they rarely bothered with any furniture other than beds. Her stepfather, whom her mother had married when Marion was eight, was something of a nomad. It was rare that Marion completed a full year at the same school.

Looking back, Marion sees that all the moving gave her the ability to adapt quickly, to succeed even when she didn't know what was around the corner, and it gave her the courage to launch and then learn in later life. But as a kid, being the perpetual new girl was a challenge, and on top of that, Marion was often the only Hispanic child in each school. She recalls one particularly upsetting time in sixth grade when she wanted to have a slumber party but none of the other parents would let their little girls come because she was different.

During her junior year in high school, Marion fell in love. When her family once again prepared to move—Marion had by that time attended seventeen different schools in twelve different school districts—she decided to stay in New Mexico and get married. Though only a junior, she was just two credits shy of her high school diploma, so she dropped out of school to start adult life with her new husband. She earned the final two credits in night school while working during the day at a tax office, the latest in a string of jobs she'd held as a teenager, including Travelodge maid, busgirl, and answering-service employee.

Even though her counselors in high school had told her that, based on her grades and standardized test scores, she could pretty much write her own ticket to any college she wanted to go, Marion decided to focus on motherhood; the pregnant girls she met in night school had given her baby fever. A month before her eighteenth birthday, Marion had her first child.

A few years later came the second child. Marion had wanted to stop at one, but her husband had pushed for a second. (Marion gave in when their priest told her she was being selfish.) But as she raised her children, the words of her counselors rang in her ears. *You could write your own ticket.*

Now living in the suburbs of Dallas with her family, Marion enrolled in a community college, where she eventually became a student instructor in the math department. When she got a scholarship from Texas Instruments, she transferred to the University of Texas at Arlington and continued working toward a computer science degree. She didn't worry about what she'd do with it—that could be figured out later. She was just happy to be excelling academically.

Then she felt the lump in her breast. It was small, but it was definitely there. The first doctor told her she was too young, at twenty-nine, to have cancer. "Cut back on your caffeine, and you'll be okay," he told her. Relieved, she went home.

But the lump kept growing, and soon her breasts were asymmetrical. Two doctors and several months later, she finally got a diagnosis that was correct but devastating: breast cancer, and, coincidentally, cervical cancer as well. She had a hysterectomy and a mastectomy within weeks of each other.

A devastating new chapter in Marion's life had begun. Strained financially—she had no health insurance—weakened by the chemotherapy, and losing her hair, she had to drop out of college. On top of it all, her marriage was buckling under the strain. Her husband's support seemed to flag as more and more of Marion's hair fell out.

Though she had no idea where life would take her, considering all these new developments, Marion trained her attention on the short term, getting a job, even if that meant quitting chemotherapy a few months early to regain her strength.

She decided to go an unconventional route: car sales. She'd worked a part-time secretarial job at a dealership a few years before and had been stunned by the salesmen's mistakes: they botched sale after sale by appealing to the male half of the couple. *Don't they get that she's the boss?* Marion had asked herself again and again.

It was the fall of 1984, and Marion began pounding the pavement, unconcerned that she didn't have any experience selling cars. She was launching, knowing she could learn later. After visits to sixteen car dealerships, she had received sixteen rejections. A few times, she'd seen the sales manager peek around the corner, see that she was a woman, and send out an assistant to say he was unavailable. But Marion pressed on, focusing on what she was going to do each day to get closer to employment.

At last she got a warm lead from a friend and went to see sales manager number seventeen. He was a progressive guy, especially for Texas. After a brief interview he leaned back in his desk chair, sizing Marion up, and said, "You know, I've been thinking about hiring a broad lately, and you seem like the nervy type."

Once she had been hired, Marion had to face the fact that she didn't know anything about car sales. But she didn't spend her time worrying about that. She just knew she could figure it out as she went along. So she threw herself into the two weeks of training the dealership gave her, absorbing everything she could.

She took to car sales like a duck to water, despite having to put up with rampant sexual harassment, intimidation, and mean-spirited competition. One car salesman literally cut her off at the pass as she made her way toward a customer, and she ended up falling into a flower bed with a broken high heel.

After two and a half years, Marion felt it was time to get off the sales floor and out of the stifling Texas heat. She took a 75 percent pay cut to move into management at a different dealership. She knew if she worked hard and learned as much as she could, it could lead to owning her own dealership someday. Sure enough, she learned the ropes of management day by day, ascended the ladder quickly, and was even able to find an investor willing to front the $800,000 she needed as starting capital for her own agency. Marion opened Love Chrysler in Corpus Christi, Texas.

Marion opening Love Chrysler

Marion at her dealership

"I knew I didn't have to figure this all out in one day," says Marion. "If I had waited to become a car dealer until I had learned all there is to know about the auto industry, I'd still be waiting today. In any profession, the yardstick is always moving.

"As I travel around the country today and speak, I'm finding that more and more women want to have their plan down pat and know everything before they start. But this just doesn't work."

Marion learned the lesson again in the financial tsunami of 2008, which hit car dealerships really hard. Suddenly, out of the blue, she was forced to find a way to pay off a $10 million loan on her car inventory in thirty days or face bankruptcy.

Rather than be overwhelmed, she took a first small step: she secured a short-term loan that stretched those thirty days to six months. In those six months, she was able to negotiate a longer-term loan, but the price was really high. Marion had to lay people off, stop taking a salary, and liquidate most of her retirement plan. Why didn't she just give up? As Marion says, "There are no for sures and there are no forevers. I've learned to replace any temptation I ever have to be a victim, the 'Why me?' with 'What now?'"

Today Marion's dealership has been profitable for two full years.

"I hear people say 'someday' a lot," says Marion. "I tell them, your someday is now. You don't have the luxury of waiting until your husband gets his promotion or you sell the house—you just have to start doing something today. Wishing and hoping is futile. If you really want to embark on something, regardless of how simple, ask yourself, 'Am I doing something every day to work toward that end?'"

LAUNCHING AND LEARNING

We know that many women don't accomplish what they want because something is holding them back, and we will explore working around internal and external limitations later in the book. But one thing that holds women back is prevalent enough to require a chapter all to itself.

One thing I constantly hear from women is "I want to do this, but I don't know how." Not knowing how to do something should never be a reason not to try, and that's where Launching and Learning comes into play. As Marion said, "If I had waited to become a car dealer until I had learned all there is to know about the auto industry, I'd still be waiting today."

I am going to fill you in on a secret. No one knows what they are doing when they start something new. Do you think Amy Sewell knew how to make a documentary or Anne Heyman knew how to create a youth village or Jacqueline Edelberg knew how to re-create her neighborhood school?

Instead, these women and most other people who accomplish something practice Launching and Learning. What that means is that you just launch your idea and then figure it out as you go along. Will you make mistakes with this method? Of course, but even your mistakes tell you something. As Indie Lee said,

> So you didn't get that one outcome, but you learned from that and then you can always change directions. It's okay to make mistakes; everyone does. I don't think life would be fun if you didn't make mistakes. I get some of the best joy out of, "Oh my gosh, what did I just do? That didn't make any sense." But who cares, because I'm doing it and I learned from it.

How I Launched and Learned with This Book

Here's how I used Launch and Learn with this project. Let's start with everything I didn't know. I didn't know how to write a book. I didn't know what I would write about. I didn't know how to find the women to profile. I didn't know how to interview the women once I found them. I didn't know how to do the survey that I used as research for the book. I didn't know how to find a publisher for a book. I didn't know how to market the book. That's just a small amount of the stuff I didn't know. And yet here I am today with a published book.

So what I did was to ignore those things I didn't know (which clearly could have overwhelmed me and caused me to give up) and just launched the project. I even announced publicly at my workshops and in my newsletter, "I am writing a book." That way it would have been tougher to back out, as people were constantly asking me, "How is the book coming?"

And then I spent each day just figuring out what I needed to learn then to move the project forward. For example, to find the women to interview, I discovered that you could post a notice on a reporter website looking for interview subjects. So I posted that I was seeking remarkable women who had done something interesting later in life. The responses were amazing, and several of those women are profiled in this book. And to learn how to interview them, I spent hours researching how to conduct an interview, including talking to anyone I knew who had ever conducted an interview (thanks to my friend Julie, who suggested I watch several *Today Show* interviews to see how the pros do it). My first interview was with Amy Sewell, and she couldn't have been more gracious, as she knew I was a novice. And then with each subsequent interview, I got a little better.

As I am writing this chapter, I am figuring out the process of finding a publisher. I am telling everyone I know and meet that I am looking for a publisher (you never know whose cousin works for a publishing house). But I still have no answers. The only publisher I have sent my proposal to so far (this was two weeks ago) turned me down so fast, it was humiliating. I emailed the proposal and within an hour (which means they didn't even consider the idea), I got a call from a woman who sounded young enough to be my daughter saying, "There are too many books out about what women want to do next, so we don't want to do this book." Ouch! Well the fact that you are reading this book means I somehow figured out the publishing issue.

I have certainly made mistakes along the way, but as I look back at the mistakes, I did learn something (just like Indie). All that these mistakes cost me were time and some money, both of which I knew upfront I could handle.

Now that you see how I Launched and Learned, let's think about how you can do this with your idea. Think again about what success looks like. What is the first thing you need to do in order to start? For Anne Heyman, it was to go to Israel to determine if there was a model she could follow. For Jacqueline Edelberg, it was to meet with the principal of her local school. For Mary Beth Knight, it was to sign up for her first race. For Marion, it was getting hired into the good ol' boys club of car dealers. So what is your very first step? Commit in your mind to just this first step (that's not so scary, is it?). And set a firm date to do it. Announce to others what you are doing. This not only provides accountability (they will ask you how you are coming along), but also you just might get some good ideas from others when they hear what you are doing. If you shy away from announcing to others, perhaps deep down you don't think you will follow through, and you don't want to be embarrassed if you don't. This is all the more reason why you must announce it, so that you will be fully committed.

And if you launch and it ends up all wrong, so what? Did anyone die? Will your kids still love you?

As we learn from 102-year-old Sara Pollak, who you'll meet in the next chapter: "If you try it and it doesn't work out, don't give up; go to something else." In other words, it's not really hit or miss, but elimination. Keep trying, and eventually you will find it.

ᏩᎧ

As you Launch and Learn, you may find that things don't happen as quickly as you want them to. Perhaps you have trouble mastering something, or an unforeseen circumstance prevents you from carrying out the initiative you launched. Sara Pollak realized that major accomplishments take time. Sara never stopped working toward what she wanted—even in old age. Her secret? Taking one step at a time, even if the next step is a very tiny one.

EIGHT

Taking Small Steps

*I did not see the whole. I only saw this poisonous snake
which I had to kill in order to take the next step. I only saw the
problem directly in front of me. If I had seen the whole thing,
I would have been too overwhelmed to have attempted this.*

—*Henry Morton Stanley, African explorer*

IN CHAPTER 1, AMY SEWELL PARAPHRASED an ancient Japanese
verse: "One inch in front of you is total darkness." In other words, you
shouldn't worry about the future; instead, focus on what you have to
do today. I agree, and that's why I recommend taking small steps to
accomplish your Act Three goals.

Sara Pollak has taken one small step after another to reach her goals
for 102 years. Yes, you read that right—102 years. Widowed during the
Great Depression when she had just had a baby, she worked her way

through school at night, and after many years she finally graduated from college. But what really sets Sara apart is that she kept moving her entire life, finally getting her PhD at the age of seventy-eight!

SARA'S STORY

The energetic Sara Pollak, who today lives independently in Cleveland, often says that her life began at forty-five. Born in 1909, she grew up in Chicago as the youngest child, with five older brothers. Although she had a happy childhood, she was afflicted with a speech impediment. At her weekly sessions with her speech therapist, a lovely English woman, Sara felt inspired. Starting at age eight, she hung on to a dream that one day she would become a speech therapist.

Sara as a child

But when it was time for Sarah to go to college, her father died suddenly. Her mother, a domineering woman whom Sara loved but clashed with, told her she didn't need an education. "All you need to learn is how to diaper a child and take care of a household." At any rate, Sara needed to earn money to support herself. She knew her speech therapy career would just have to wait. She just didn't realize for how long.

Taking a job at the University of Chicago, Sara earned enough to feed herself and pay for a few classes in the morning—tuition at the university in those days was $50 a quarter. She and her coworkers would make potato pancakes together when they got off at 9:00 p.m. (that was all they could afford to eat), and in the mornings Sara would exchange 25¢ for a big bowl of hot oatmeal that would hold her for quite a while.

In her third year at the university, her friend Henrietta introduced Sara to her twin brother. Henry became the love of Sara's life, and soon after they met they got married. If she wanted to have a fight with him, he'd say, "Let's sleep over it, and tomorrow morning we'll fight about it." Sara reports that by the next morning she would have forgotten about it, so they never had a fight in the two years they were married. Sara was soon expecting their first child. But after little Mark was born, she came down with childbed fever—an often-fatal condition. After three weeks in the hospital, Sara had weakened. Though she weighed only ninety pounds, she was allowed to go home, but only with the assistance of a nursemaid and a housekeeper. It was three months before she was back on her feet, and by then the medical bills were staggering.

Henry, concerned for his wife's health, decided to drive home late at night; he'd been on the road overseeing the force of sixteen salesmen he managed. Around midnight, he fell asleep at the wheel, ran off the road, and was immediately killed in the crash.

Sara, deep in debt, found herself in a state of shock that lasted years. She packed up baby Mark's things and prepared to move back into her childhood home, but only before issuing an ultimatum to her mother: "The day I say, 'Mark, do this,' and you say, 'Mark, you don't have to,' that's the day I'm moving out."

Eventually Sara was able to go back to work, and she took a job that allowed her to build her skills in accounting. The old dream of speech therapy was still with her, but accounting was what paid the bills—even if she hated it every step of the way.

And she did hate it. In fact, her sleep was increasingly filled with nightmares. In them, she frequently found herself in a room with no doors or windows, trapped, unable to escape. When she started walking in her sleep, she knew it was time to see a counselor.

In one of her first sessions, she explained to her counselor that she wanted to go back to school and eventually wanted to be a speech

Sara in her forties

therapist. She concluded with her biggest fear: "But I'm almost forty."

"So what?" said the counselor.

That night at home, Sara thought, *He's right. So what?* "Those were the two most important words of my life," says Sara. "The following week I went and registered for classes at Northwestern in speech therapy."

Sara had taken the first small step toward a new phase of her education, but her life didn't get any less hectic: she was going to school in the mornings, working in the afternoons, and taking care of Mark in the evenings. She cooked a week's worth of dinners every weekend and froze them for each night of the week. She commuted from the south side of Chicago to Evanston every day, using the hour-and-a-half ride to study.

At Northwestern, she met Felix, the man who would become her second husband. He was Jewish, a poet, and a curator of rare books, and he had fled Vienna during World War II. From the day he approached Sara in the Northwestern library and asked her to a play, she was enthralled with him. Both struggling financially, the two ate brown-bag lunches by the lake almost every day. Six months later, they were married.

By now, Sara had received her degree. At Felix's urging, the small family moved to Madison, Wisconsin. The University of Wisconsin had an excellent speech therapy program, and Sara was ready for her next launch: a master's degree. Comfortably living on Felix's salary, Sara became a TA and took a full schedule of classes. At forty-five, she graduated and became a licensed speech therapist, finally taking steps toward the career she'd pictured for herself.

For twenty years, she worked with both children and adults, sharing the gift of speech that she'd been given decades before. One client grew to be a symbol of the fulfillment her work brought her. A child was referred to her, and as was her custom, she visited the family at home to talk about how best to stimulate the child's speech. When the door opened, she was greeted by the boy's father, dressed in a full firefighter's uniform. He welcomed her in, and as she discussed the boy's difficulties, Sara noticed the father's heavy lisp. Before she left, the father said, "Miss...you may have noticed I have a speech defect, too."

He went on to explain that he'd been a dispatcher for years but was unable to rise in rank because of his speech. Sara met privately with the man twice a week for two years. He worked hard, and she didn't charge him a dime. His speech vastly improved as a result of their sessions, and the man eventually rose to become assistant fire chief.

At age sixty-six, Sara retired to take care of Felix, who'd lost his eyesight and needed care. Many women might've been disappointed. Many women might've settled for a quiet life at home. But Sara continued taking steps forward. Post-retirement, she coauthored a book on language interaction in the classroom, developed teacher-training materials, and conducted workshops in ten different states.

Sara had also kept up a zest for learning well into her seventies, taking the occasional class and attending lectures on art, music, literature, her own field—anything that sparked her interest. She didn't harbor any thoughts of going back to school full-time until one day, at age seventy-five, as she sat at a late lunch with a former colleague. "What are you going to do now, Sara?" her friend asked.

Without thinking, she replied, "I think I'll take a PhD."

Good to her word as ever, Sara enrolled in a doctorate program, where she studied with fifteen thirtysomething students. Sara reports this "as the most stimulating time of my life." Three years later, Sara, at age seventy-eight, was fielding questions from the entire faculty as she defended her dissertation. Her adviser asked her to wait outside the room for what seemed to Sara an interminable amount of time. Finally, her adviser stepped outside, looked her in the eye, shook her

Sara in cap and gown for PhD

hand, and said, "Congratulations, Dr. Pollak." Sara was overjoyed. "Even now when I think about it, my whole being just gets infused.

"The fact that people are afraid to try new things interests me," says Sara. "You wonder why. What is there to be afraid of? You can fail, but at least you tried. If you try it and it doesn't work out, don't give up, go to something else. Moving in any direction eventually leads you to the right place."

Sara feels that she just kept taking steps forward to finally achieve what she had wanted. "In fact, I told my son and my grandchildren that they shouldn't mourn me when I die because I have fulfilled my life. And how many people have fulfilled their lives? They could if they really tried."

LEARNING TO TAKE SMALL STEPS

I am a big fan of the TV show *The Biggest Loser*. I love to watch people tackle what seems to me to be an overwhelming challenge and then succeed. In one episode, one of the contestants had to lose 300 pounds! Anytime he thought about the fact that, as he said, "I have to lose a whole person," he'd get really discouraged. I mean really, how do you wrap your head around that kind of challenge? So he'd want to give up and quit because the long-term goal seemed too insurmountable. Bob, the trainer on the show, gave this contestant really good advice: "You can't think about that. Just think about what you need to do tomorrow. The rest will take care of itself."

Doesn't that make sense? Why worry about whether you can ultimately hit the big scary goal a month or a year down the road—whether it's losing 300 pounds; finding a job as a cancer-stricken single mother, like Marion in chapter 7; or getting your PhD, like Sara—when really what you need to push yourself through is just that one step you need to take tomorrow. That step is probably something more manageable: running a mile to lose two pounds, drafting a resumé and doing some job market research, or getting a short-term loan.

Now, you may be wondering, if that's the case, then why in chapter 5 did I ask you to visualize your long-term goal? Long-term goals are important so that you know what you are aiming for, like losing 300 pounds or, in my case, sitting on Oprah's couch. But now is not the time to think about that goal. Remember what Terry, the master visualizer, said in chapter 5, after she'd "released" her vision: "If you don't focus on *now*, that vision isn't going to happen,"

The first reason for setting aside the long-term goal in favor of small steps is that it allows you to avoid feelings of hopelessness. It's easy to convince yourself that your objective is unattainable, especially if there's a wide gulf between where you are and where you want to be.

I was recently coaching a woman who was going through a divorce. She was totally overwhelmed by the process and the prospect of having to go back to work after being at home for thirteen years, raising her children. We did the visioning exercise from chapter 5, and she could visualize herself working in a supportive office environment, but there were just so many hurdles to cross to get there that she already felt like giving up. We talked about what would be the very first step she needed to take, just one step. It turned out that she had been putting off telling her children about the impending divorce because she was uncertain of the best way to do it. Telling them, she decided, would be her first step, and we strategized about how she would figure out the best way to do this: by reading books, by meeting with a therapist who specialized in divorce issues, and by speaking with her lawyer. She wrote me the next day to say she had already been to the bookstore and had scheduled a meeting with the divorce therapist. Again, taking one step at a time helps you avoid hopelessness.

The second reason for setting aside the long-term goal in favor of small steps is that you get fully comfortable with each small step before undertaking the next one. Humans are hardwired to want to feel comfortable. If we are too uncomfortable and feeling too much stress, we will do anything to avoid feeling that way. (Think of the last time you walked into a cocktail party full of people you didn't know. If you felt uncomfortable, your natural inclination was to want to get out of there.) Feelings of stress and discomfort will occur if you try to do too much, too fast. To avoid those feelings, the easiest thing is to quit. But instead, if you take just one small step at a time, getting comfortable along the way, you have a much higher chance of success.

Here's an illustration of this fact. I decided to take a swimming lesson as I figured that a few suggestions from a coach could help. Very early on in the lesson, I knew I was in trouble. The instructor changed everything about my swimming style, from the way I held my hands to the way I kicked my feet. She even changed how I breathed. I spent the entire lesson overwhelmed by how bad I must be and how hard it would be to improve. I took in so much water while trying that I literally and figuratively felt I was drowning.

I considered just giving up and going back to my old way of swimming. But then the idea came to me. I coach my clients to take one step at a time and to get comfortable with each step before moving—why wouldn't that work here?

So the next time in the pool I decided to focus on just three things: holding my hands like flippers, keeping my head down, and using my arms in the proper motion. It still felt uncomfortable, but at least I wasn't drowning. And the next time I got in the pool, those three things actually started to feel more natural. So I added another suggestion—keeping my arms at shoulder width as they entered the water. Again, initially it felt strange, but after several laps, I could see that I was swimming a little faster. I repeated this throughout the summer, adding one suggestion each time I swam, and now I am a totally different swimmer.

I think this story so clearly illustrates why taking small steps is the best way to avoid those awful feelings of discomfort that can cause you to give up and retreat back to your comfort zone.

Many of the women whose stories we've heard so far mastered the art of taking small steps. Anne Heyman stands out—what she calls "step-by-step" project management was a particular strength of hers, enabling her to organize the challenging project of a Rwandan youth village piece by piece. "It was not the way project management is supposed to happen," says Anne.

In typical project management, you'd have the entire project mapped out. But here I just took it one step at a time. First, we put together this group to go to Israel to see what the model should be. Then we looked at land in Rwanda. Once we looked at land, I was willing to talk to architects. Once I'd found an architect, I was willing to talk to builders. But I wouldn't be pushed faster than we could move, one step at a time. I think the only way to have done this is step by step. If I had looked at the whole picture I might never have done what I did. But by taking it piece by piece, perhaps it didn't get overwhelming.

EXERCISE: MAKE A SMALL-STEPS LIST

Thinking about your own vision, you may feel overwhelmed about how far you need to move from where you are now and how much you might need to change. This can be discouraging. Maybe you wonder if you can do anything significant at your age, or with your background, or with your finances, or with your health condition. The key, as Marion Brem puts it, is to go from "Why me?" to "What now?" Rather than wallow in where you are, release the negativity and take a look at the first baby step you can take.

To help yourself do this, make a list of all the steps you need to accomplish in the next month. Notice that I said in the next month and not all the steps you need to reach your goal. Most of us can't begin to know all the steps we are going to need to take to reach our goal. But we can probably figure out what we might need to do in each month. Then each month redo the list, crossing off what has been accomplished and adding new steps for the coming month. This works really well with Launching and Learning, which I described in chapter 7. Each next step will become apparent as you learn as you go along. If a monthly list seems overwhelming, scale back to a week. If that's still too much, map out what you need to do in the next two days. It doesn't matter how many small steps ahead you've planned—it just matters that you plan them and then keep taking them.

To help you see what I mean, here is the small-step list compiled by my client Elizabeth. Elizabeth decided that she wanted to become a social worker, for which she'd need a master's degree. Elizabeth was actually able to make not just a one-month step-by-step list, but a seven-month list, ending with enrollment in her master's program. Here is her seven-month list.

MONTH ONE

1. Meet with admissions officers of all five local universities to find out about their master's programs.

2. Evaluate curriculum, tuition costs, job placement help.

3. Meet with a graduate of each program.

4. Learn about taking the GRE.

MONTH TWO

1. Pick top two university options out of the five.

2. Begin application for top two choices.

3. Register for and start studying for GRE.

MONTH THREE

1. Finalize application for top two choices; get it in on time.

2. Study for GRE.

3. Get recommendations done.

4. Get university interviews done.

MONTH FOUR

1. Study for GRE.

2. Take GRE.

MONTH FIVE
OFF

MONTH SIX

1. Visit each school (assuming accepted to both).

2. Choose school.

MONTH SEVEN

1. Start school.

You can see that this process took Elizabeth seven months. I am not saying that taking small steps requires this many months; that's just how it worked out for her. If this was a job search, and not conditioned on a school calendar, the time frame could have been significantly compressed. The key is not how long your list is, but that each step is thought out, written down, made manageable, and then, most important, completed.

⁍

As I surveyed women for this book, I was overwhelmed by how many respondents mentioned the need for flexibility as something that was holding them back from stepping into Act Three (we'll go into that more deeply in chapter 10). As you're looking at these months-long schedules, maybe you're thinking the same thing: *Will I be able to fit a big, all-consuming goal into my already-busy life? I've got a lot going on, and I like my "me time"!*

But embarking on your third act doesn't mean giving up flexibility or having laser focus on a single big-picture goal. In fact, the great thing about this phase is that women are often able to achieve fulfillment without sacrificing their freedom and free time. How? By creating a Portfolio Career, which we'll look at in the next chapter.

NINE

Creating a Portfolio Career

*The woman who can create her own job
is the woman who will win fame and fortune.*

—*Amelia Earhart*

LAST WEEK, I WAS STANDING BEHIND a woman at the counter of an ice cream shop. She kept asking the server to sample lots of different flavors. And then she couldn't decide which she wanted from all the various choices. It was as if the plethora of choice had paralyzed her. Finally, I butted in: "How about taking some of each?" It seemed like a perfectly reasonable solution to me.

What do you do when you are in an ice cream store and can't pick just one delicious flavor? Do you get stuck and just walk out thinking,

Well, if I can't have all the flavors I want, I won't pick any? And yet that is just what some women do when they can't settle on just one thing to do—they don't do anything. In the ice cream store, you can ask for some of each. And you can do the same thing in creating a fulfilling life. I call that having a "Portfolio Career™"—where you pick a variety of different projects that you like to do or perhaps need to do to make money, or for some other reason, and collectively this portfolio of activities creates a fulfilling life for you. And the best part of a Portfolio Career is that it can give you the kind of flexibility many women crave.

Dayna Steele, Houston's "First Lady of Radio," lived out her dream of being a DJ for almost two decades. Steele spent years traveling, seeing shows, and interviewing countless rock stars—names like Bono, Ozzy, Bowie, Jagger.

But when she lost her DJ job and had her first child in the same week, Dayna had no idea where to go next. Instead of ramping up for a huge reentry into the industry she'd always worked in, Dayna mixed and matched the things she loved and was good at to create a Portfolio Career.

DAYNA'S STORY

Dayna Steele was so ambitious that she felt ready to start her career and move into her own apartment by the time she was twelve. The daughter of a gregarious mother and a business-savvy, risk-taking father, Dayna enjoyed her upper-middle-class childhood in Houston. In ninth grade, she started taking correspondence college courses during the summer, earning enough credits to head off to Texas A&M a year early.

She started studying premed—"it sounded important," she remembers—but was thrown off course when she went to a party that was also attended by a DJ from a local Top 40 radio station. He was like a star to Dayna, and she was completely enamored. As she chatted with him, she smiled, touched his arm, left him openings to ask her out. He never asked, but Dayna, spurred by her crush, started DJing at Texas

Dayna on the air as a teenager

A&M's student station in College Station, Texas. The moment she put on those headphones, she knew she'd found her calling.

A couple of months into her stint on college radio, Dayna caught wind of a Top 40 station in College Station that was about to get hit with an EEOC lawsuit—it didn't have any women on board. Dayna called them. She was the only woman in a hundred-mile radius who was licensed and willing to work for next to nothing.

Once she skipped her first class to be at the radio station, it was hard to stop. She found she was happiest not in the classroom but at the station, even if she wasn't on the air yet.

At eighteen, Dayna saw an ad for a sales secretary position at a radio station back home in Houston. She applied, fudging a bit by saying she could type. She figured she'd fake it until she learned (remember Launch and Learn from chapter 7).

She got the job, quit college, and moved back to Houston. But within days of starting, she already hated it. She was doing grunt work and was forced to work alongside the DJs she wanted to be like without getting a shot at it herself.

Headstrong Dayna, still a teenager, decided to take matters into her own hands. Suppressing her nerves, she knocked on the program manager's door and asked to be put on the air if the opportunity arose. He basically patted her on the head and dismissed her, but her request would pay off sooner than she'd even hoped.

That night, the phone at her apartment rang. It was the program director. "So you want to be on the air?" he asked. The DJ who was supposed to cover the 9:00 p.m. to 6:00 a.m. shift hadn't shown up for work. Danya could tell from the noise in the background that the director and the other DJs who could've taken over had been drinking and getting high and certainly weren't in a condition to be on the air. She drove to the station and manned the booth until 6:00 a.m., and that was the beginning of her twenty-year on-air career.

When the station switched formats—from rock to disco—Dayna's filling-in role turned into a full-time DJ position on the graveyard shift, midnight to 6:00 a.m. A few months later a pop station, one of the most successful in the country, called her up and offered her the 7:00 p.m. to midnight shift. She took it.

From there, Dayna was on her way to the pinnacle of her profession. She was quickly promoted to music director and assistant program director. She was being wined and dined by music executives and flown around the country to big-name shows at clubs she couldn't legally get into yet; they'd often have to sneak her in through the back door. If there was a hot event, Dayna was there—in the VIP section.

She was surrounded by heavy drinking, but alcohol was never tempting to Dayna. Drugs were another story. She got into cocaine for a few years in the eighties—it came with the territory of hanging out with rock stars. Fortunately, she was able to stop before it got out of control: "I have this inner compass," says Dayna, "like an inner guidance system. So I just decided I couldn't do the drugs anymore. It was too crazy."

Dayna had struck up a friendship with David Crosby of Crosby, Stills, and Nash, and he called her one day and asked her to arrange the transport of a group of astronauts to an upcoming show. In the back of a limo sent by Atlantic Records, surrounded by a bunch of guys from NASA, Dayna met Charlie, a pilot who would become her husband and best friend. They've been together since that night.

Five years later, Dayna was pregnant. She was ecstatic, but she found herself at a crisis point. She couldn't come to an agreement with the station over maternity leave, and when they looked at what Dayna was pulling down—$150,000 a year—they told her to take a hike.

*Dayna as a "pregnant cover girl," imitating
the famous Demi Moore Vanity Fair cover*

Dayna was jobless and expecting, ousted from the job that had defined her life for more than a decade.

After a few years of doing hit-and-miss radio work elsewhere,

Dayna found herself back on her feet as host of a popular talk radio program. But when the station announced an upcoming format change, Dayna decided to throw in the towel. "I didn't want to work that hard at something where the rug could be pulled out from under me when stockholders weren't happy," says Dayna.

It was time for something that would give her more freedom and variety. Dayna began constructing a Portfolio Career. She got a contract doing freelance PR work for a friend. She spent time on The Space Store, a website she'd founded to sell astronaut-themed merchandise that earlier had been

Dayna Steele

available only at the Kennedy and Johnson Space Centers. She started giving speeches about what she'd learned in her career, spicing up her early, shakier appearances with Van Halen stories. She wrote a book, *Rock to the Top: What I Learned About Success from the World's Greatest Rock Stars*, with a foreword by Gene Simmons.

"When people ask what I do, I say, 'Everything,'" says Dayna. "I do lots of things that pull from my many talents and strengths. When you put it all together, it makes for a remarkable life."

"A lot of people think they have to find one job, but you really don't. I do crisis communication, consulting, aerospace social media. I do tons of oil company DVDs—sales DVDs for blowout preventers, mega-wells, etc.—and I'm an author and speaker."

Dayna's put together a variety of interesting projects that add up to a fabulous, flexible third act. She's ditched the business suits and high heels in favor of jeans and rock 'n' roll T-shirts. And she makes room for everything she enjoys, whether it's running a website, sharing stories of her days in radio, enjoying time with her sons, or spending a quiet hour doing laundry—something she sincerely likes to do.

As Dayna puts it, "Life is more fun when you get to do something different every day."

CREATING YOUR PORTFOLIO CAREER

Dayna created a great Portfolio Career that allows her to use her talents doing many she things loves, all the while retaining her flexibility, and you can, too.

A Portfolio Career is a mix of activities or jobs that at the end of the day leads to a meaningful life. Don't get caught up on the term *career* by thinking, *Well, I don't want a "career," so this must not be for me.* The portfolio can be made up of paid or unpaid projects or jobs.

Like Dayna, I have the perfect Portfolio Career. Yes, I am the president of Act Three, but I also run my own women's conference called Imagine . . . Then Do It. I am a keynote speaker at other women's conferences, am a writer, serve on several nonprofit boards, am an adjunct professor of business law, manage some real estate, and teach or rehearse ballet. I feel lucky each week to get to do such a variety of interesting things. For some of you, the fact that I do all these activities may sound overwhelming, but it works for me mostly because I have empty-nested. The advantage of a Portfolio Career is that you can add and subtract as your personal situation requires. At the time that my youngest child started driving, I added the Imagine conference, and once he left for college, I began writing this book.

A Portfolio Career isn't for everyone. You have to enjoy juggling lots of different balls at the same time and switching gears pretty quickly. On any given day, I might send a rental agreement for my real estate work, start preparing for an upcoming speech, and coach a client. The next day I might teach a ballet class, go to a community meeting, and have lunch with a sponsor of my Imagine conference. If this kind of schedule with lots of different activities sounds chaotic to you—as compared to fun—chances are you'd be more satisfied with a traditional, more focused approach.

If you're finding yourself drawn to the idea of a Portfolio Career, maybe you had a difficult time visualizing your Oprah moment. Portfolio Careers, by their nature, aren't easy to encapsulate in a single pinnacle moment. If you struggled with the visualization exercises, go back and try them again, this time keeping your mind open to working simultaneously on a variety of projects.

The truth is, anyone—male or female, young or old—can create a Portfolio Career. But it's an approach that's especially well suited to many women who are moving out of full-time motherhood. "Time is one of the gifts of this stage of life," says Dayna. "You have skills you have built up over the decades, and now you have the gift of time. That's a great combination to create a life that you care about."

EXERCISE: THE PORTFOLIO CAREER PIE CHART

To take your current life and start moving it toward a Portfolio Career, it helps to first understand where you are currently spending your time. Then you can layer on the projects and ideas that came out of your Power Equation in chapter 4—the elements you want to include in your life.

STEP 1: LIST YOUR WEEKLY ACTIVITIES.

List all the activities that do in a typical week; include things like grocery shopping, exercise, cooking, reading, tennis, manicures. Don't leave anything out, even if you think it is insignificant, but exclude sleeping and eating. It may be helpful to carry around a notebook for a few weeks recording what you do. It can be a shocking surprise when you review this list after a few weeks and actually see where your time goes. I had one client tell me she had no idea she talked to her mother on the phone for that many hours a week.

STEP 2: GROUP THE ACTIVITIES INTO CATEGORIES OF YOUR CHOICE.

Yours might be something like

- *groceries, cooking dinner, and errands*
  —"home stuff"
- *carpools, going to kids' sports games, and homework help*
  —"kid stuff"
- *reading, watching TV, surfing, and talking on the phone*
  —"leisure"
- *showering/drying hair, getting nails done*
  —"grooming"
- *tennis team, spin class*
  —"exercise"
- *PTA, soccer coach, church work*
  —"community"

STEP 3: QUANTIFY THE TIME YOU SPEND ON YOUR ACTIVITIES.

Assign the number of hours in a week you spend on each category. It doesn't need to be exact—just get as close as you can. Translate those hours into the percentage of time spent on each category.

STEP 4: CREATE YOUR PIE CHART.

Create a pie chart based of the percentages. You can do this using Microsoft Excel, or you can just draw it. Here's the chart of one of my clients. The category names were determined by the client when she grouped her activities:

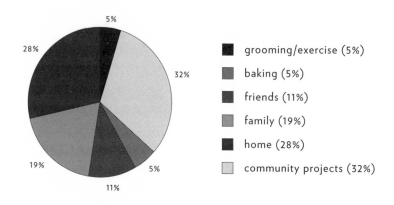

HOURS SPENT PER WEEK
ON VARIOUS TASKS AND PROJECTS

- grooming/exercise (5%)
- baking (5%)
- friends (11%)
- family (19%)
- home (28%)
- community projects (32%)

STEP 5: IDENTIFY THE PROJECTS AND IDEAS FROM YOUR POWER EQUATION THAT YOU WANT TO INCLUDE IN YOUR PORTFOLIO CAREER.

The next step in creating a Portfolio Career is to identify those projects and ideas that you would like to be able to include in your life, and then approximate how much time you would need each week to accomplish this. For example, the client with the pie chart shown above had a Gifted Passion of gardening and a Gifted Passion of helping disadvantaged children succeed. In doing her Power Equation, she decided that for her Gifted Passion of gardening she wanted to teach classes at a local gardening center, and for her Gifted Passion of helping disadvantaged children, she wanted to be trained to be a CASA volunteer to help foster children. She believed that she needed to spend ten hours a week on each of these projects.

STEP 6: REDRAW YOUR PIE CHART TO MAKE ROOM EACH WEEK FOR YOUR NEW PROJECTS/IDEAS.

In order to have the time to spend on these new projects, other current activities obviously need to be discontinued or pared back. I had one client who cut back her weekly manicure to every two weeks, dropped two (out of her six) weekly workouts (including travel time and showering), and had a neighborhood senior bring her daughter home from school two days a week. With just these small changes, she saved seven hours a week.

In order to make time for her new gardening and CASA work, my client whose pie chart is shown above stopped baking, spent less time with friends, and eliminated one current (and less than fulfilling) community project. We redid her chart adding the two new activities and deleting what she had chosen to delete. This is what it looked like.

HOURS SPENT PER WEEK ON VARIOUS TASKS AND PROJECTS (REDRAWN)

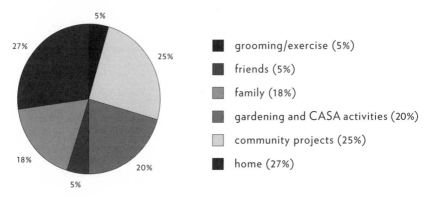

- grooming/exercise (5%)
- friends (5%)
- family (18%)
- gardening and CASA activities (20%)
- community projects (25%)
- home (27%)

How would you add a few Gifted Passions into your schedule? You might want to start with one and gradually add others until you have the kind of flexible Portfolio Career you deserve, just like Dayna and me.

To help you visualize what your Portfolio Career pie chart might look like, here is a pretty extreme example—my current Portfolio Career pie chart. I mentioned above all the different activities I do in a given week. Well, this is how it looks, and for me personally, it's a very fulfilling life.

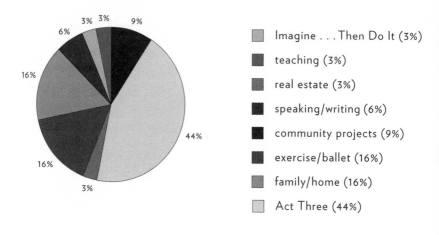

JULIE'S HOURS SPENT PER WEEK ON VARIOUS TASKS AND PROJECTS

Legend:
- Imagine . . . Then Do It (3%)
- teaching (3%)
- real estate (3%)
- speaking/writing (6%)
- community projects (9%)
- exercise/ballet (16%)
- family/home (16%)
- Act Three (44%)

Regardless of whether you're better suited to a Portfolio Career or a single, focused endeavor in your third act, you're likely going to experience some initial reluctance when you embark on your Act Three. Many women feel discouraged at this stage in their lives; over and over I see women who put off third-act happiness because something is holding them back, whether it's internal doubt or an external situation. Let's take a look at some of the most common things that prevent women from stepping boldly into their Act Three and how you can deal with those things.

TEN

What's Holding You Back?

*I believe that anyone can conquer fear
by doing the things he fears to do.*

—*Eleanor Roosevelt*

IN ORDER TO BE ABLE TO move forward in your third act with confidence, it is important to identify all the things that can sabotage success, whether they are attitudes you have about yourself or objective, external barriers keeping you from achieving what you want. We already discussed in chapter 7 one of the most common success spoilers: not knowing how to do something, which is addressed by Launching and Learning. This chapter will help to flesh out those issues that could derail progress before they occur.

Annie Wilder, empty-nesting at the age of thirty-six in Wisconsin, decided it was time to pursue her dream of being a writer. Casting off the fear that would have held many women back, Annie quit her office job and started cleaning houses to make more time for her writing. Hers is an encouraging story of not letting anything hold you back— even a live-in ghost!

ANNIE'S STORY

"I'm pregnant." They were the two hardest words fifteen-year-old Annie Wilder, the third of eight children in a large Catholic family, had ever said. The plan had been for Annie to do what her siblings had done: go to college, take a year or two to travel, land a respectable job, and *then* marry and have a couple of kids. Now all that was out the window. Her parents were less than thrilled, but they supported Annie as she made plans to have her baby, continue with high school, and marry the eighteen-year-old father of her child.

Annie today

By age seventeen, Annie had gotten her GED and had her second child. By the time she was eighteen, she and her husband had saved enough money to sell the trailer they had been living in and buy a modest home in Wisconsin. The family of four lived comfortably on her husband's salary and the income from an insulation company the couple had bought together. Annie, still a teenager, did the company's bookkeeping when the kids were napping.

Soon her marriage began to falter. The first time her husband hit her, Annie was eighteen. She gave him another chance, thinking he couldn't really mean it, since they loved each other. But her husband began to spiral out of control. He even was in five car accidents in the last year and a half of their marriage.

Annie was scared and not sure where to turn. She wanted to start taking college courses, hoping she could finish her degree before the marriage ended. She approached St. Catherine's, a small Catholic women's college, which was reluctant to admit her since she hadn't completed high school.

"What can I do to prove I'm ready to do this?" she asked an administrator. "How about if I take some tests?"

The school agreed, and Annie took a test that would give her probationary admission to St. Catherine's. When she returned a week later to meet about her results, an admissions officer informed her that she'd been accepted, as long as she took no more than two classes at a time and maintained a high GPA. When the officer left the room momentarily, Annie noticed a folder with her name on it sitting on the desk. Glancing back toward the door, she quickly opened it and saw that she'd gotten fifty-nine out of sixty questions correct—and that the average score was forty-five correct questions. She closed the folder as a huge smile spread across her face.

Annie's marriage finally ended in 1986. She hadn't finished college, but she'd jumped from freshman to junior in one year by testing out of classes. That was a big help, since she barely had enough money to cover tuition. A single mom at that point, she cleaned houses and

watched other people's children until she achieved her communica-
tions degree from St. Catherine's.

From there, Annie took up a career at a human services agency. The
pay was terrible, but she stuck it out, rising from an entry-level position as personnel coordinator to become HR director and corporate
office manager seven years later. As she built her career, she was nour-
ished by the rewards of day-to-day parenting. Her son and daughter,
growing rapidly from toddlers to preteens to full-fledged teenagers,
were the center of her life.

When her daughter, Molly, turned eighteen and was preparing to
leave home, the implication weighed heavily on thirty-four-year-old
Annie. She knew she'd measured up as a parent, but what was next?
"I had to step into something else that was important and good so that
I didn't crash and cling onto my kids," says Annie. "They were ready
and prepared to start their own lives. I needed to get ready and set up
something of my own."

She toyed with the idea of being a psychologist or a lawyer, but a
nagging voice urged her to pursue a passion that had lain dormant for
years: writing. Annie had a gift with words and had sent out some work
in her twenties, but everything had been rejected. She knew, however,
that if she got to the end of her life and hadn't given writing a fair shot,
she'd regret it. Undaunted by the fact that she had no idea how to make
money as a writer, Annie said good-bye to her colleagues at the agency
and returned to cleaning houses.

You might think that Annie would have trouble telling people she
cleaned houses for a living—after all, she was a young woman who'd
worked hard to get her college degree and who'd risen through the
ranks of the working world. But Annie wasn't about to let other people's perceptions throw her off course. "I like to clean," she says. "It's
peaceful. I was only cleaning for people I liked, and I was going to see if
I could regain enough inner peace to write."

Annie was now empty-nesting, cleaning houses by day, writing in
her free time and . . . living with a ghost. She was then living in a groovy
old house that had always been one of her dreams. A few years before,

when Annie had been house hunting, one day her realtor called and told her that there was a house that had just come on the market. It was an old Victorian. "When we toured it, you felt like somebody was right in the room watching you, and my realtor felt it too," says Annie. "There was a ghost here. Actually there were lots of ghosts but one main ghost—the old guy who had lived there before. Apparently he had buried money in the basement in a dirt room, and I believe that's one reason why he stuck around." She immediately bought the house.

When Annie moved in she didn't mind the presence at all. She even joked that perhaps the ghost would finally leave after all these years just to get away from her son the Elvis impersonator. Years later, as she began writing again in earnest, she actually found the environment inspiring.

The first professional writing she did was movie reviews for a local progressive newspaper—she'd struck up a conversation with the editor of the paper at a hippie potluck she'd gone to with a friend. They liked her reviews enough to ask her to write a front-page story on the dating scene in the Twin Cities. Then came other articles in the progressive paper and in regional tourism magazines.

Annie's writing muscles were stretched and strengthening as she neared the end of the second year of her working sabbatical. There was just one problem: she was running out of money. *I want a full-time writing job*, Annie told herself. *And I want it by the time I'm forty.*

Despite not having any specialized training in writing, Annie beat her deadline when a friend told her about a copywriting job at a publishing company and Annie landed it.

Annie was happy working in the marketing department of the publishing house, reading books and writing the copy that would convince shoppers and bookstore owners to take notice of them.

One day she sat at her desk reading a manuscript submitted by a woman from New York. In it, the woman described the spooky goings-on in her creaky old house. Annie couldn't help but be reminded of her own haunted home—the faint tapping on the walls; the heavy, gloomy presence she sometimes felt. She'd even had some guests report unexplained gusts of cool wind or quick tugs on their hair. *I could totally*

Annie's house

write something like this, she thought as she read the manuscript and drafted the descriptive copy.

About a year later, she was doing just that. Undeterred by her inexperience in book writing, Annie landed a contract to write a book about her home and pounded out a manuscript in three months.

Annie was elated when the book was published and actually started selling at a brisk pace. Part of her was reluctant to put herself out there and state her belief in the presences that lived in her home, but she didn't let it hold her back. She didn't even flinch when she went on TV and told her interviewer that, yes, a ghost had actually put its tongue in her ear. As Annie says, "I guess I just have an ability to put aside the fear of embarrassment. When I need to convince myself to push through something difficult or intimidating, I just remind myself, 'Nobody is really paying that much attention to you anyway.'"

Now Annie is working on a third book and responding to interest in adapting her work for a television show. She hardly took the conventional path to becoming a published author, but she was able to look at the things that could hold her back, whether it was an unexpected pregnancy, a failed marriage, apprehension about quitting her job and going full-speed-ahead toward her dream of being a writer, or even a ghost.

"I don't let fear of failure stop me," says Annie. "I guess my philosophy is that I'd rather try and fail, because to me that's not failure. To me failure is not trying. As long as I'm trying, I'm moving ahead. I don't give away my power based on what other people think of me. Whatever I want to do, I ask myself, 'How will I get there?' I'm just not wired to wait for permission."

STRIKING AT THE ROOT OF WHAT HOLDS YOU BACK

When I say to women, "If you want to make a change in your life, why haven't you done it?" many answer that they simply don't know what they want to do. That's often true, but it doesn't fully answer the question. As we've seen, every woman has an interest in something, and no matter how long she's been at home, no matter how old she is, every woman has an aptitude for something. If women really investigate why they aren't making changes, many would find that it's not that they don't know what they want. What's really going on is that something is holding them back.

Annie is an incredible example of someone who didn't let circumstances hold her back from her dreams. So many times she could've been restricted by what was going on around her—teen pregnancy, rejection from schools, fear that she didn't have enough writing experience or money to pick up a new career after raising kids. Annie knew what was holding her back, and she overcame it.

When you take the time to think about what's holding you back, some really interesting thoughts can occur. It's quite likely that something you didn't consciously realize is restraining you. Here are some examples culled from material that clients have written when asked to really think about what might be holding them back.

So, with tears, I have had to fully face the roadblock of fear as well as the embarrassment of its existence. Now I must operate knowing it is there. Often this fear is very tricky and will show up as self-doubt, busyness, focusing on everyone else's needs, complaining, and fatigue. It is my responsibility to recognize this and keep moving. It's not rocket science, and it certainly is not a big challenge relative to what most people face in their lives. But it is my challenge of the moment, and I must own it with help from coaches, mentors, and friends.

❧

I have anxiety that I will be taking time and/or money away from my family for something that might not even be successful or lucrative.

❧

For me, I have a significant personal issue (weight), which keeps me stagnant and unwilling to take chances until I figure out why I haven't addressed that issue.

❧

I am afraid that if I fail, I will look like a failure to others. Right now, I'm a good mom, homemaker, and wife. Those things are going well, so my life looks successful even though I feel like I am missing something. But if I try something new and fail, that good impression of me will be shattered.

❧

My belief that my happiness is relatively unimportant holds me back. My husband's and/or kids' happiness is the most important, or even the only thing that's important. I have had a difficult time asserting my needs/wants for happiness and not ever feeling validated in going after it. When I was working, I felt much less like this. I had typical insecurities and doubts about my abilities, but in general I felt much better about myself and my self-worth. Somewhere in the last fourteen years of staying home with kids, I have lost a lot of my feelings of self-worth, self-confidence, and self-esteem.

⟲

I am a breast cancer survivor. This is a major obstacle for me—that I hope just temporarily has knocked me off my life's path. Dealing with illness—your own or that of a family member—can take the stuffing out of a person (hopefully temporarily). I think one of the measures about great women is what they do after they have dealt with what life dishes out.

Do any of these feelings resonate with you? Here are some other typical reasons that women feel hold them back from pursuing their third act:

A SPOUSE. In my survey, 19 percent of women agreed that their spouses would hold them back from pursuing their next stage. When a wife has been handling all the household demands for many years, her husband may be unhappy about changing his way of life to pick up the slack as she becomes busier with outside activities. I had one client tell me that her husband, a busy doctor, wasn't interested after all these years in renegotiating their sharing of "chores." His response was "Why should I have to do more so that you can make $30,000 a year, which we don't really need?"

Another challenge for a successful husband is that typically, just as his wife is empty-nesting and ready to launch, he might be interested in slowing down and taking more time off to travel and enjoy life—and he wants her with him.

This dilemma is shown poignantly in the movie *Barney's Version.* Barney, played by Paul Giamatti, is married to a beautiful and highly educated woman named Miriam, played by Rosamund Pike. Miriam gave up her career in radio when they started to raise a family. As her oldest son leaves for college, Miriam and Barney have lunch together and Miriam describes to Barney how much she wants to go back to work, that she now feels a strong desire to pursue her dreams. His response is that he'll take early retirement, and then they can travel or even go live in Italy together. He feels threatened by her returning to work and fearful of other men whom she might meet and find more worthy than him. Miriam tells Barney, "This is not about you—this is about me." Eventually, they divorce as Miriam moves ahead in her life and Barney can't adjust to this new version of his wife.

JULIE THE CRUISE DIRECTOR SYNDROME. Remember the TV show *The Love Boat*? And remember the cruise director, Julie? My client Renee coined the term "Julie the Cruise Director Syndrome," defining it as "being so involved in everyone else's life that you avoid focusing on your own." In my survey, 37 percent of women agreed that they used their family's needs to avoid thinking of their own. They can justify to themselves that they really are much too busy to even think about what else they could be doing. But the reality is that deep down, they know this is just an excuse to avoid thinking about their own futures.

DESIRE FOR FLEXIBILITY. Eighty-four percent of the respondents to my survey agreed that a fear of losing their flexibility was holding them back. When women say they don't want to give up their flexibility, what they really mean is that they don't want to give up control of their schedule—doing what they want, when they want. After being home for ten, fifteen, twenty years raising kids and being in complete control of their own schedule (my husband is going to a conference in San Diego; why shouldn't I go too), it is really difficult to think about committing to something that might require giving up that control. For many women, this issue becomes a nonstarter, stopping them dead in their tracks when they haven't even considered all the various ways to both get the life they want and the flexibility they crave.

FEAR OF RUSTY SKILLS. Forty-two percent of respondents to my survey told me that it was a fear of rusty skills and inability to compete that held them back. This is actually one of the easiest issues to solve. If a child came home from school complaining to her mother that her skills weren't good enough to make the tennis team, what do you think that mother would do? Of course, she'd be on the phone in ten seconds flat signing her daughter up for tennis lessons. But when it's about the woman's own rusty skills, she shies away from doing the same, whether its signing up at a community college to improve computer skills or going away for a weeklong course covering today's global marketing issues.

EXERCISE: FINDING OUT WHAT'S HOLDING YOU BACK

With these examples to pull from, it's your turn to determine what is holding you back. Take out a piece a paper and a pen and ask yourself the questions "If I could do anything that I wanted to do, what would stop me? What would get in my way?" Now write everything that comes into your head for the next five minutes. Nothing is too insignificant to consider (not even "I have to be home at 2:00 to let the dog out"). If you feel okay about sharing your restraints with a close friend, it can be fun to brainstorm with another person.

Then think of ways to address each of the items on your list. If you have to walk the dog at 2:00, the solution could be hiring a neighborhood kid to do it for you. If you don't want to give up flexibility, you could choose to seek out project work rather than a new full-time endeavor. If you have Julie the Cruise Director Syndrome, the solution could be saying something like this to family members: "In order for me to move forward, I need to stop getting involved unless I'm critically needed, so please help me to do that." If you worry that your skills are rusty, the solution could be signing up for a class that will address areas where you feel deficient.

The point is that, with creative thinking, there is a solution to almost every issue.

And if you can't find a solution, perhaps this isn't the time to move forward. This is the second benefit of exploring the things that hold you back: sometimes you have limitations that actually do preclude certain courses of action. If your spouse is truly opposed to a project and you want to avoid ending up in a divorce, you'd need to evaluate whether it's worth being held back. Maybe it's time to put your project on the back burner while you do some marriage counseling. If you have four small children, a sick parent, or a husband who just got transferred, day-to-day life may simply be standing in the way—for the time being, at least. Remember, timing is everything. If life is truly holding you back at the moment (and the key word here is "truly"), then it may not the best time to make major changes—but that doesn't mean you need to give up on them. Just focus on continuing to get in Change Shape, preparing for the day when the restraint you're dealing with can be thrown off.

√

There are generally two types of obstacles that women encounter as they go through Act Three. There are the preexisting conditions that make you reluctant to do the things that will bring you happiness— that's what we've been talking about in this chapter.

The second kind of obstacle is the kind that presents itself once you've set out on your third act: the kinks in your plan you couldn't possibly have imagined. I'm not going to sugarcoat this: you *will* come up against difficulties, no matter what you pursue in your Act Three. To be successful on your journey, you must learn how to anticipate and deal with them.

In the next chapter, we'll look at some strategies to do just that— right after we hear from a famous woman who overcame a potentially career-ending third-act obstacle with extraordinary grace.

ELEVEN

Persevering Through Setbacks and Overcoming Obstacles

Nearly every man who develops an idea works at it up to the point where it looks impossible, and then gets discouraged. That's not the place to become discouraged.

—*Thomas A. Edison*

Success consists of going from failure to failure without loss of enthusiasm.

—*Winston Churchill*

THE OTHER NIGHT I WAS WATCHING *The Biggest Loser* on TV again. This was the first week of a new season and therefore the first week that these new contestants, all weighing between 300 and 400 pounds, were introduced to the gym. It was totally incredible to me to watch how hard these people were working. One woman passed out, one man puked, but they never gave up. They just got back up and kept pushing themselves, one foot ahead of the other on the treadmill. Granted, they had Jillian yelling at them, which certainly helped give them the impetus to keep going, but the real desire, this amazing perseverance, had to come from within. I think the reason I was so impressed by their perseverance was the fact that until they got to the show, they obviously had none, and I mean zero perseverance, or they wouldn't have ended up weighing so much. Their weight was not due to a few extra brownies; it was from many years of having zero ability to persevere in living a healthy lifestyle.

How does one go from zero perseverance to persevering through such pain and adversity that it actually makes you puke? We'll explore that in this chapter (though of course I'm not advocating that you push yourself until you puke). Developing that ability to persevere through something difficult is important to reaching your goals in your third act of life.

Diane Rehm is one of the most respected interviewers in media today. Diane was a stay-at-home mother living in Washington, DC, when she walked into the door at WAMU to volunteer for a little radio program she'd heard about. That volunteer position turned into *The Diane Rehm Show*, which is listened to by millions of people every day. She had to persevere to get to that point, but Diane's real test of determination came after she was well into her third act.

DIANE'S STORY

Diane Rehm grew up in 1940s with one foot in the Arab world and one in the American world, and she says she could literally feel the difference as she left her house to walk to school. Her father and mother, both immigrants from the Middle East, believed that girls were not to be heard. For Diane to question her parents, speak back to them, or even express opinions of her own would've been unthinkable. Her voice wasn't exactly welcome.

On the other hand, the moment young Diane stepped outside her house, whether into the classroom (where her hand was always the first up) or into her friends' houses, she was eager to display her knowledge and curiosity. It was, in fact, outside of her house that Diane was able to make ample use of her voice. She took roles in community theater, developing a deep love for the stage. And at the age of sixteen, while Diane was working for the director of the DC Department of Highways, she got her first experience speaking over a radio—when the director asked her to relay pothole information to the guys in the field over the two-way radio.

Diane, age eighteen or nineteen

When she graduated from high school and broached the topic of college with her parents, their reply was firm: "No way." They didn't have the money to send her, and they expected her to marry and have children right out of the gate.

So following what was expected of her, Diane, at nineteen, married an Arab man eight years her senior. Her mother tragically succumbed to a long illness two months later, and her father passed away ten months after that. Diane believes he died of a broken heart.

Diane's husband expected her to be a traditional Arab wife. She was to cook, clean, and submit to the dictates of the Syrian Orthodox church, which seemed to govern almost every area of her life. She felt stifled. At one church meeting that had been dominated by men, Diane stood up and spoke, ignoring her husband's efforts to tug her back into her seat. "I was not allowed to speak as a child," says Diane, "and darned if I was going to go through life as an adult not speaking."

In the third year of her marriage, she asked for a divorce. It was a difficult thing, especially for her husband. His family and their Arab community had never seen a divorce, but Diane felt she had to get out.

Living on her own in an apartment was a new and frightening experience, as she had never even spent a night alone before, but she carried on. She'd been recruited from the Department of Highways to the Postal Inspection Service to the State Department with a good raise. At the State Department, she met a young lawyer named John Rehm, who would become her husband and life partner. John's first image of Diane, seated behind a desk with some of her favorite books—by Dostoyevsky, Albert North Whitehead, and Somerset Maugham—surprised him as being rather unusual for a secretary. They were married a year later, in December 1959.

As Diane built a life with John, she filled it with the things that brought her happiness: music, sewing, volunteering, and friendships. In the following years, two children came along, Jenny and David. Diane was thrilled.

Yet as the years passed, she was plagued by persistent feelings of self-doubt. She'd never gone to college—something that weighed on

Diane, John, and her kids, 1966

her heavily at times. Added to this was her feeling of pent-up energy. She knew she could be doing more. Diane heard from a friend about a program called New Horizons offered at George Washington University, designed to assist women like her in figuring out how to spend the rest of their lives. Just picking up the phone to call and ask about the program filled her with trepidation.

"What the program did initially was not great," Diane remembers. "About a hundred and twenty women signed up. They put the women with the PhDs on the top floor, the ones with master's degrees on the next floor, bachelor's on the first floor, and the rest of us in the basement." Needless to say, this didn't soothe her insecurities about her education.

Nevertheless, Diane was delighted to find herself in a group of women confronting the same situation she was. Sitting in the basement, exchanging visions and plans for the future, the women came to the consensus that Diane should be in broadcasting. "Where did that come from?" says Diane. "I don't know."

Soon thereafter, Diane was volunteering with the Hospitality and Information Service, which offers assistance to the wives of diplomats visiting the nation's capital. The wife of a Canadian diplomat mentioned that she was volunteering at a little radio station, WAMU-FM. "Honestly, if you could've seen me that day, you would've seen a light bulb go on over my head," Diane says. "I thought, *Wow, volunteering at a radio station. Do you suppose . . .*" The diplomat's wife asked the station if they'd be open to an additional volunteer, and the host, after meeting with Diane, said she'd like her to come back the following Monday.

When Monday rolled around, Diane was beyond scared. "I thought the host was going to kick me out," she remembers. "She will think I'm dumb; she will think I don't know what I'm talking about or doing; she won't like my suggestions." So Diane stood in front of the mirror at her house and gave herself a pep talk, saying out loud over and over again, "Put my fears aside, and no one must know how scared I am."

Once she got to the station, things got even scarier. The host of the radio show was out sick, so WAMU's manager was going to take over the show for the day. The manager shocked Diane when she suggested that Diane be on the air with her. Looking back, Diane agrees that being on the air on her very first day really was astounding. She remembers that the guest that day was a representative of the National Dairy Council. She felt surprisingly comfortable and confident. "I just jumped right in," says Diane. "I mean, come on—I'm a mother. I've been at home for fourteen years, I know about this stupid Department of Agriculture food pyramid that's all wrong." At the end of the broadcast, Diane was elated—her third act was taking root, all because she had overcome her nerves and misgivings and volunteered at WAMU.

For ten months, Diane volunteered at WAMU, thinking of her time there as an apprenticeship, a chance to delve into an area she didn't know and to learn from people she respected. When an actual paid job as an assistant producer opened at the station, Diane was afraid to apply, fearful of the risk of a "real" job. It was her husband, John, who really encouraged her, and she was overjoyed when she got the job. Diane's career snowballed from there, eventually leading to her own radio show called *Kaleidoscope*, which was renamed *The Diane Rehm Show* in 1984. To the outside world, Diane appeared to be supremely confident, but she was still battling strong feelings of inadequacy, feelings that she was really just a great pretender. "I had this fear of failure, concerns simply of going into the studio every day feeling as if I was not going to make it. It was every single day," says Diane. "There's really nothing you can do except put one foot in front of the other."

Behavioral therapy helped Diane stomp down her tendency to expect the worst. But the true test of Diane's ability to persevere came to a head on a Monday morning in February 1998. Diane had been struggling with a strange voice problem for weeks—unpredictably, her voice would get raspy and halting. Diane had begun to worry daily

Diane and Al Gore at the station

about whether it would hold up for one more show. On that Monday morning, she was at the ballroom of a Four Seasons, surrounded by 350 people, moderating a panel titled "Gossip: What's America Talking About?" Her voice started faltering, with a vengeance. She imagined the audience wondering how she ever got a job speaking on the radio. She spoke as little as possible, waiting until the end of the session to run back to WAMU and tell her boss she needed a break.

Radio hosts' fortunes are, obviously, tied directly to their voices. This was a devastating blow for Diane. At first, her therapist told her that her voice issues were her body's way of telling her to lessen her stress. This might have caused many to give up. She didn't accept this diagnosis and finally traveled to Johns Hopkins, where the condition was accurately diagnosed as spasmodic dysphonia, a condition that interferes with the messages sent from the brain to the vocal cords, causing the vocal cords to clamp down inappropriately.

For a while, her voice was the first thing Diane thought about each morning. She was losing sleep and analyzing every tiny irregularity of her speech. She had to come up with a solution or never go back on the air. Fortunately, spasmodic dysphonia is treatable—Botox injections to the vocal cords temporarily improve the problem. But the injections don't fix it, as is apparent from Diane's distinctive voice today.

"To get over that fear of going back on the air after those months and people wondering what's wrong with my voice and why I am on the air, was very difficult," Diane recalls. "People are used to my voice now, but it's a hurdle every day, because I know how I sound. I don't kid myself, but I tell myself that what's important is the tone and topic of the program. People now say they love my voice. I just say thank you and keep putting one foot in front of the other."

LEARNING TO PERSEVERE THROUGH OBSTACLES

At the beginning of the chapter I asked the question, "How does one go from zero perseverance to persevering through such pain and adversity that it actually makes you puke?" Developing that ability to persevere through something difficult, as Diane did in dealing with her voice challenges, is important to reaching your goals in your third act of life.

First, I want to clarify how persevering through obstacles is different than something that might hold you back, which we discussed in chapter 10. The distinction lies in the timing. In anticipation of your third act, you can think about the things that might hold you back and plan around them, but you can't know the obstacles until you've launched and hit one. In order to understand this distinction, let's use Diane as an example. If I had asked her prior to embarking on her third act, "What might hold you back," her answer might have been that she didn't have a college degree, she didn't know what she wanted to do, and she needed to be home by 3:00 when the kids got off the bus. If instead I had asked her, "What obstacles did you persevere through to get to where you are today?" her answer might have been the feelings of failure that she had to overcome every day to walk into the studio, dealing with spasmodic dysphonia as a radio host, and now dealing with her husband's deteriorating health. And Diane isn't the only one of the women in this book to overcome obstacles: think of Indie Lee with her brain tumor, Marion Brem with the financial meltdown of the car industry, and Mary Beth Knight getting back into shape after a C-section. These are all unforeseen obstacles that each woman needed to overcome. In fact, every woman profiled in this book has persevered to get to where she is today.

Everyone has her own way of dealing with obstacles, whether it's simple hard work or a shift in attitude. I loved something Annie Wilder told me: when someone tells her she can't do something she says, "Oh yeah?" and gets a new wave of determination. She uses naysayers as a way of getting motivated to overcome the roadblocks ahead of her. Inspiring!

NINE STRATEGIES FOR PERSEVERING

So how do you develop the ability, as Diane has, to persevere through something difficult? Here are nine helpful tips.

1. ASK YOURSELF, IF YOU'VE LOST THE ABILITY TO PUSH THROUGH A DIFFICULT CHALLENGE, TO PERSEVERE. Take a good hard look in the mirror and ask yourself when was the last time you set a long-term goal for yourself and then actually stuck to the program until you reached that goal.

If you can answer that you see things through to the end most of the time, then great, perseverance is not a big issue for you. But if you are like many of my clients, the ability to really stick to something is gone. When you were younger, you probably were able to see things through, so what happened? What happened is that you are out of practice. Your life has gotten a little too easy and you have become complacent (and if you are really honest with yourself, you know I am telling the truth). Your life is just good enough. Financial insecurity can counteract complacency, but most of my clients and the women I surveyed are financially secure (with the exception of my divorced clients). Being accountable to a boss can also counteract complacency (like Jillian, the *Biggest Loser* trainer, yelling in your ear). But most of my clients don't work, so it's been years since they were truly accountable to someone else in a professional sense. Even though my clients may wish things were different and wish they felt more engaged and fulfilled, they often find that it's too easy to quit when they hit bumps in the road. The first step, then, is to recognize that this is an important issue.

2. BELIEVE IN THE END RESULT. You really have to believe in what you are doing. Remember when I told you in chapter 7 how the first publisher that I sent my book proposal to called me so quickly to reject it that it made my head spin. That was a big bump in the road, and it would have been easy for me as a novice author to assume that they must be right and to give up before I got too far along in writing the book. But I really believed in the end result, that there was a need for this book (contrary to that publisher's opinion), and so I spent the five weeks after the rejection writing furiously to finish it. Making sure that you truly believe in the end result (and reminding yourself of that often) will help you to persevere.

3. RECOGNIZE THAT THERE WILL BE BUMPS IN THE ROAD. When you are walking through a haunted house at Halloween, which is scarier, the ghost that you see up ahead that jumps at you and says "boo" or the one that you can't see behind the corner that jumps out and surprises you? Of course, the ghost that surprises you is much scarier. Well, it's the same with bumps in the road. If you are expecting that there will be bumps, then you won't be surprised when you hit one. You may not know yet what the actual bumps will be, but the fact that you will hit them is a certainty. Make this your mantra: "I will hit big and small bumps along the way." Then when one comes along, you can think, "Well, I was expecting a bump, and, boy, is this a big one." It doesn't seem so scary when you are expecting something, and reducing this fear will allow you to persevere.

4. MAKE A COMMITMENT—TO YOURSELF OR AN ACCOUNTABILITY PARTNER. When you say you are going to do something, what percentage of things do you actually do? I call this the "say/do ratio." I admire people who do what they say they will do, and I assume you do, too. So make the commitment to yourself that you will be one of those people who will see a plan through.

It helps to make this commitment not just to yourself but to someone else as well. When you say it out loud, it makes the commitment more real. The other person can then hold you accountable to your commitment (as perhaps a boss would). When you face a challenge, the other person should listen to your complaints and doubts but then encourage you to keep moving, providing the accountability that many of us need to succeed.

Who should you pick for the job of accountability partner? Well, a spouse may not be the best person. Do you really want your husband admonishing you when you aren't making the progress you should? That is not necessarily the best way to continue a great relationship. Besides, some spouses can even have an unspoken desire for you to *not* succeed, that can be hurtful to your progress. Perhaps a better choice would be a good friend whose judgment you respect. Plan specific monthly accountability meetings with this friend where you review the progress you are making and discuss any hurdles. Some people find it helpful to actually have a group of friends, in effect a board of advisers, who not only provide accountability but also can serve as sounding boards and provide good advice.

But what if you don't have a friend you want in this role? Well, there are even websites where you can post your goals online and be accountable to the world. StickK.com is one of many. Some of these sites even force you to put up money, which you lose to charity if you don't meet your goal. Now that's an added incentive! When I last went to StickK.com, I saw goals as varied as "Finish my thesis by September" to "Finish a painting every month" to "Spend ten minutes a day on my future."

The bottom line: when you've made an official commitment to do something, you're much more likely to overcome the obstacles you'll meet on the way.

5. GET IN CHANGE SHAPE. If you are already in Change Shape (see chapter 6) at the time that you hit an obstacle, you will sail through it more easily, with less disruption. Think of a pregnant woman delivering her baby. That's a pretty challenging event. If she is in good physical shape right up to the delivery, in most cases she is going to have an easier delivery and will return to her pre-pregnancy condition more quickly than a woman who has spent nine months on the couch eating bonbons. The same holds true for moving into your third act. Get in Change Shape and the mountains you have to overcome will feel like small bumps.

6. DON'T TREAT EVERYTHING AS A BIG OBSTACLE, OR "DON'T SWEAT THE SMALL STUFF." Author Richard Carlson writes in his book *Don't Sweat the Small Stuff . . . and It's All Small Stuff* that "often we allow ourselves to get all worked up about things that, upon closer examination, *aren't* really that big a deal." He is exactly right. We can use an enormous amount of emotional energy blowing things out of proportion. And in my experience, women tend to do this more than men. So don't make something a big obstacle when it really isn't. When what appears to be a big barrier comes your way, ask yourself this very important question: "Am I going to care about this problem in a year?" If the answer is yes (think of Indie's brain tumor), then this is an obstacle worth worrying about. If the answer is no, take a deep breath and think about how to keep it in perspective . . . almost everything is just small stuff.

7. GET A COACH. There's a reason millions of people work with a coach each year. It works. A coach can ask you the tough questions to make your success more likely, can provide advice, can help you stay motivated, and can help you strategize how to push through roadblocks. I suggest that you find a coach who is certified by the International Coach Federation (ICF). Unfortunately, today there is no requirement that a person be certified or have any training whatsoever before calling themselves a coach, and many people who may or may not be qualified advertise themselves as coaches. Finding a coach who is certified by the ICF at least ensures that the coach has training. I have personally gone through this certification training and found it to be of very high quality.

8. MAKE A "WORKAROUND PLAN" EACH TIME YOU HIT A ROAD-BLOCK. I love how 102-year-old Sara Pollak did this. Here's what she told me:

> In life, there are many roadblocks, constantly. What you have to do is push through, and if you can't go through something, you have to learn to go around it. When I decided to go back for my doctorate, that was a very big roadblock because my husband was completely blind. How do you deal with taking care of him, going to school, and taking care of a house? What I did was not give up. I worked it out. I went to

school in the morning and then arranged to be home by noon when he was up. So the way I handled the roadblock was to look at it, decide it was something I really wanted, and figure out my way around it.

If you have a challenge, spend time coming up with all the possible ways to work around it or otherwise deal with it, as Sara did. You should already have some practice thinking of ways to work around challenges from chapter 10, when I asked you to consider all the things that could hold you back.

9. ASK OTHERS FOR HELP. When you hit a roadblock, ask yourself, "Who can help me succeed?" For example, if you've been sending out your resumé to find a new job for several months and not getting the response you want, that's a pretty big reason to ask who can help you overcome that situation.

Many women shy away from asking for help because they have the misconception that asking illuminates their lack of knowledge or self-confidence. But I will let you in on a little secret. I am the queen at admitting I don't know how to do something and asking for help. I have found that people are surprisingly gracious and happy to share their knowledge. Here is just one example culled from many experiences with this book project. You may recall that I mentioned in chapter 7 that I had no idea how to interview a person. I had never had any journalism training, and I didn't even know how to record the interviews. Yet doing these interviews correctly was a critical success factor for the book. So when I first got Amy Sewell (whom you met in chapter 1) on the phone months prior to our actual interview, I asked for suggestions. She didn't know me, so why did she help me? Because I admitted that I needed help, and she had expertise and experience to share. Will everyone help? Probably not, but most people will. You won't know unless you ask them.

And for those situations where you really need an expert, my very strong suggestion is to buy the best help you can find. If you want to overcome an obstacle, you may need to spend some money to do so.

View this as an investment in yourself. I find that some women shy away from this investment, as if they feel they aren't worth it. If that sounds like you, ask yourself this: If your child struggled with math, would you hesitate to hire a tutor to help him overcome this challenge? Of course not. So why would you invest in your child and not in yourself?

☙

Getting started on the road to Act Three is a thrilling experience. You're brimming with possibilities for the future. You're discovering new abilities and passions, or you're dusting off old ones. But then you hit your first problem—a gap in funds, an illness, a stubborn family member, a web of red tape to cut through. If you want to make the most of this new stage of your life, it's imperative that you learn how to not succumb to the disappointment that comes with these obstructions. You'll probably want to throw up your hands and say, "This isn't at all what I thought I'd be dealing with!"

Don't. Use the strategies above to get a better handle on the situation. Once you're overcoming obstacles on a regular basis, it will be like a new skill—one that enables you to build a gratifying and fulfilling Act Three.

Conclusion

IN THE INTRODUCTION I ASKED YOU to pretend that you are eighty years old and looking back at your life, and then to ask yourself the questions "Was this the life I wanted? Has this life been fulfilling?" I asked you to ponder these difficult questions because the startling answer of "no" can serve as that wake-up call, that catalyst to start now making the necessary changes so that someday you can answer "yes."

Hopefully, through explanation, exercises, and the inspirational stories of our Act Three women in each chapter, you now have a better sense of how to create your fulfilling Act Three.

Amy Sewell taught us how to dream big.

Anne Heyman taught us how to find our Gifted Passions.

Jacqueline Edelberg taught us how to discover our motivations.

Indie Lee taught us how to combine our Gifted Passions with our motivations.

Terry Grahl taught us how to visualize success.

Mary Beth Knight taught us how to get in Change Shape.

Marion Luna Brem taught us how to Launch and Learn.

Sara Pollak taught us how to take small steps to achieve our goals.

Dayna Steele taught us how to create a Portfolio Career.

Annie Wilder taught us to consider what's holding us back.

Diane Rehm taught us to overcome adversity.

I wish that all of you will someday be able to feel like 102-year-old Sara Pollak: "I told my son and my grandchildren that they shouldn't mourn me when I die because I have fulfilled my life." Isn't that really what all of us want?

I'd love to hear from you. Please let me know how you are using the ideas from this book to create your fulfilling Act Three. You can email me at admin@actthree.com. I will be collecting these stories for my blog.

If you'd like coaching help from the great coaches at Act Three to help you figure out what you want to do next and how to get there (we coach women just like you across the country), email us at admin@actthree.com for more information.

If you'd like me to be a keynote speaker at your women's conference or deliver our Discovering Your Act Three workshop, email me at julieshifman@actthree.com or call our office at 513-351-1800.

If you want to continue your exploration and share your thoughts with other Act Three women, join the conversation on our Facebook page at www.facebook.com/actthree and follow me on Twitter@actthree.

And be sure to regularly check our website for new articles and sign up for our monthly newsletter at www.actthree.com.

So here's to your Act Three!

Julie Shifman

About the Author

JULIE SHIFMAN IS AN INSPIRATIONAL, award-winning speaker, author, and business owner. Julie believes in every woman's ability to challenge herself and to grow as Julie herself continues to do. She started her career as a professional ballet dancer and then became a highly successful lawyer in New York City and Cincinnati before founding her company, Act Three, in 2008. She recently received the pres-  tigious Athena award from *Cincy Magazine* and was named a "Woman to Watch" by the *Cincinnati Enquirer*.

Through the story of her own personal transformations—from ballerina to law partner to stay-at-home mom to business owner—and through the stories of the remarkable women she has interviewed, Julie energizes women to live their best lives. She speaks with passion, humor, and heart as she encourages women to **imagine** what's next for them, and then to take one small step at a time to **do it**.

Julie is the founder and president of Act Three (www.actthree.com), an organization that helps women define their next stage of life and create their own personal action plan for living out that life. In addition to writing *Act Three: Creating the Life You Want*, Julie has also created a documentary film featuring many of these incredible women.

Visit www.youtube.com/myactthree to watch videos of Julie describing her work and inspiring other women. You can reach her at julieshifman@actthree.com or 513-351-1800.